CASE STUDIES IN
CULTURAL ANTHROPOLOGY

GENERAL EDITORS

George and Louise Spindler

STANFORD UNIVERSITY

AMISH CHILDREN

Education in the Family, School,
and Community
Second Edition

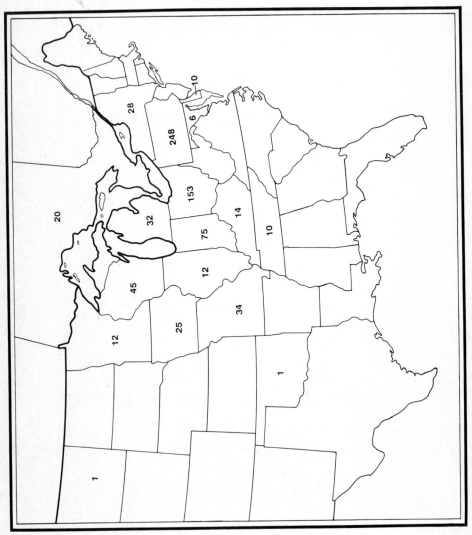

Old Order Amish Schools in North America, 1990.

AMISH CHILDREN

Education in the Family, School, and Community

Second Edition

JOHN A. HOSTETLER

GERTRUDE ENDERS HUNTINGTON

Harcourt Brace Jovanovich College Publishers

FORT WORTH PHILADELPHIA SAN DIEGO NEW YORK ORLANDO AUSTIN SAN ANTONIO
TORONTO   MONTREAL   LONDON   SYDNEY   TOKYO

Publisher	Ted Buchholz
Acquisitions Editor	Christopher P. Klein
Project Editor	Cindy Lavin
Production Manager	Thomas Urquhart
Art & Design Supervisor	Vicki McAlindon Horton
Cover Designer	Vicki McAlindon Horton

Cover photograph used by permission of Richard Reinhold.

Library of Congress Cataloging-in-Publication Data

Hostetler, John Andrew, 1918–
    Amish children : education in the family, school, and community /
John A. Hostetler and Gertrude Enders Huntington. — 2nd ed.
      p.   cm. — (Case studies in education and culture)
    Rev. ed. of: Children in Amish society. 1971.
    Includes bibliographical references and index.
    ISBN 0-03-031592-1
    1. Amish—Education—United States—Case studies. I. Huntington,
Gertrude Enders. II. Hostetler, John Andrew, 1918– Children in
Amish society. III. Title. IV. Series.
LC586.A45H67 1992
377'.8973—dc20
                 91-31733
                 CIP

ISBN: 0-03-031592-1

Address editorial correspondence to: 301 Commerce Street, Suite 3700, Fort Worth, TX 76102

Address orders to: 6277 Sea Harbor Drive, Orlando, FL 32887
1-800-782-4479, or 1-800-433-0001 (in Florida)

Printed in the United States of America

2 3 4 5   016   9 8 7 6 5 4 3 2 1

Foreword

ABOUT THE SERIES

These case studies in cultural anthropology are designed for students in beginning and intermediate courses in the social sciences, to bring them insights into the richness and complexity of human life as it is lived in different ways, in different places. The authors are men and women who have lived in the societies they write about and who are professionally trained as observers and interpreters of human behavior. Also, the authors are teachers; in their writing, the needs of the student reader remain foremost. It is our belief that when an understanding of ways of life very different from one's own is gained, abstractions and generalizations about the human condition become meaningful.

The scope and character of the series has changed continually since we published the first case studies in 1960. We are concerned with ways in which human groups and communities are coping with the massive changes wrought in their physical and social environments in recent decades. We are also concerned with the ways in which established cultures have met life's problems. And we want to include representation of the various modes of communication and emphasis that are being formed and reformed as anthropology itself changes.

We think of the CSCA as an instructional series, intended for use in the classroom. We have always used case studies in our teaching, whether for neophytes or advanced graduate students. We start with case studies, whether from our own series or from elsewhere, and weave our way into theory, and then turn again to cases. For us, they are the grounding of our discipline.

In the time since the first edition of this case study appeared in 1971, the Amish have moved further toward complete control of their schools. With the consolidation of once-separate rural schools, the tensions between the Amish community and values supporting it and the increasingly more bureaucratic and standardized school system were intensified. These tensions erupted into open confrontations that are described in this study. The Amish, with some help from their friends and some favorable court decisions, have been able to establish their own schools, maintained and paid for by the Amish communities and in school buildings most often built by Amishmen.

Schools are important boundary-maintaining mechanisms for the Amish. An Amish youth who goes beyond the eighth grade is no longer an Amish man or woman. The school teaches what one needs to know to flourish in the Amish community. The school is not only an integral part of the community, it is its penultimate expression. Schools everywhere serve as expressions of the community, though usually not as clearly. The Amish school system illustrates graphically that children can be successfully educated by teachers of their own minority group who have only informal education beyond eighth grade. Children educated in Amish schools actively participate in their own subculture and contribute to the health of American society.

When the Amish met up with a monocultural public school system that would not permit them to be raised both as Amish and as American they went their own way. In various ways most minority groups in America have experienced the same confrontation. Our school systems are in disarray because we have not found the solution to the problem of monocultural education versus multicultural school populations. It is the most pressing educational problem today, and not one to be solved by fiat. It is not clear that America can survive as a multicultural society. It is clear, however, that schools must work better for minority youth than they do, on the whole, at present. The Amish solution is not a practical one for all of America, but it is one model and it has worked well in the Amish context. The greatest value of this case study is the thoughtful description and analysis of how and why this model works and how it relates to the larger problems that we face in our time in our society.

ABOUT THE AUTHORS

The authors, both of whom are competent students of Amish culture, have combined their skills to produce this study in socialization. John A. Hostetler, Professor of Anthropology and Sociology at Temple University, was born of Amish parents in Pennsylvania and in late adolescence exceeded the bounds of his culture by obtaining higher education. He holds a Ph.D. degree from the Pennsylvania State University, has done field work in rural communities in the United States and Canada, and as a Fulbright Scholar studied the origins of communitarian societies in Switzerland and Germany. He is author of several books, including *Amish Society,* and is coauthor with Gertrude Enders Huntington of *The Hutterites in North America.*

Gertrude Enders Huntington, an anthropologist, was born in Wooster, Ohio, and now lives in Ann Arbor, Michigan, where she is a lecturer in anthropology and environmental studies at the University of Michigan. She attended Oberlin College and was graduated from Swarthmore College. She pursued graduate studies at the University of Rochester and at Yale University, where she received a Ph.D. degree, writing her dissertation on the Old Order Amish community. After teaching school in Wyoming, she taught abroad for two years at the Amerikan Kiz Koleji in Istanbul. Her role in the Amish socialization project, of which John A. Hostetler was project director, was that of resident participant-observer in the community she had observed earlier for her doctoral study.

ABOUT THIS CASE STUDY

This case study describes a way of life in which families are still stable, people live with a high sense of communal obligation, men and women work with their hands, one hears the clop of horses' hoofs rather than the squeal of tires, and the school and the community are joined. The Old Order Amish schools are taught by teachers who have no more than an eighth-grade education as far as formal schooling is concerned. In their customary one-room schools they teach "correct knowledge" rather than critical thinking. Schooling among the Old Order Amish is primarily concerned with the development of a Christian character. The properly educated member of the Old Order Amish community values cooperation and humility rather than competition and pride in achievement.

The Amish community and school present a substantial challenge to the basic assumptions and goal orientations of American society and its educational system. In the outside world academic achievement is important. Knowledge for its own sake is significant. Education in the outside society is concerned with a great many things that are unrelated to either an individual's private life or his job. The Old Order Amish see this kind of schooling as detrimental to the relationship between the individual and the community.

It is inevitable, given the divergencies between the Old Order Amish community and its schools and the communities and schools of the outside world, that there should be serious conflict. The struggle to keep the schools under their control is one of the dramatic and often heart-rending aspects of contemporary Amish life. The nature of these conflicts is also a commentary on the inability of the majority society, as represented by school officials and state legislatures, to accept deviance.

There is much to be said about the reasons for and the effects of an education in the Old Order Amish schools. The authors, John Hostetler and Gertrude Huntington, have said most of it in a careful but often forceful way. The reader will be able to judge for himself whether and on what terms the Old Order Amish education is effective. As the authors point out in the last chapter, the "how" and "why" of Amish education have many implications for other minorities in conflict with the majority society and its monolithic educational systems.

GEORGE AND LOUISE SPINDLER
Series Editors
Calistoga, California, 1991

This pony and other farm animals are an important part of the life of Amish farm children. (Photo by Richard Reinhold.)

Acknowledgments

A grant from the United States Office of Education (Project No. 6-1921) entitled "Educational Achievement and Life Style in a Traditional Society" helped to make this study possible. The authors wish to thank Wayne Miller, James Landing, Fred Buchanan, Joseph Stoll, David Luthy and many Amish parents, teachers, and school board members for their assistance and cooperation. For technical assistance we thank Gloria Basmajian, Muriel Kirkpatrick, and Jamel Williams for making the map.

Contents

1 / Amish Culture and Educational Goals

INTRODUCTION

At seven o'clock on a cold winter morning, Rebecca Miller walks across the meadow, through the heavy blanket of snow. As she approaches the one-room school building and two outhouses surrounded by a white fence, she takes out a key and unlocks the schoolhouse door.

Rebecca is nineteen years old. She teaches in Meadowbrook School, one of several hundred Old Order Amish schools in the United States. Inside, the room is cold. With trash paper and corn cobs, she lights a coal fire in the potbelly stove. In an hour, the stove gives off a cheery warmth and her pupils begin to arrive.

As the children arrive she greets each by name; "Good morning, Reuben," she says smiling, "Good morning, Lydia." During the school day her "scholars" will work quietly at their desks, individually completing their assignments in arithmetic, spelling and reading. Each child will be ready to recite when the class is called. The teacher will conduct classes for each of the eight grades in this school room. There will be a break for morning and afternoon recess and an hour for lunch time at noon.

Thirty children in eight grades sit in the bright, sunny schoolroom at Meadowbrook. The boys wear suspenders to hold up their dark broadfall trousers; the girls wear plain dresses with long aprons. There is no patterned cloth, only solid colors: blues, greens, purples, and browns, accented by black shoes. Many of the girls wear black head-coverings over neatly braided hair. Four second-graders are at the recitation bench taking turns reading aloud as the other children work quietly at their desks. The teacher listens to each child read and then, while the third grade comes up to the recitation bench, she calls on the students whose hands are raised, directing each questioning pupil along the proper path of learning.

Water drips from the wet snow on the eaves of the schoolhouse, each drop making a soft spatter as it hits the fertile ground. Along the muddy lane, water trickles in a temporary stream, fed by the melting snow. A frog pipes, the birds sound like spring. Rolling fields with an occasional grove of trees stretch towards the horizon. The distant clip-clop of a briskly trotting horse is symbolic of a way of life that needs the small rural school for the education of its children. No pavement, neither road nor sidewalk, can be seen from the schoolyard; the whine of cars and the noise of trucks on the nearest state route do not reach the schoolhouse.

Reuben glances at the clock ticking on the schoolroom wall. Soon the teacher will announce afternoon recess. From his seat he can see that the juncos have not yet flown north, for several are outside the window near the feeding station. He listens to the wind. Today they cannot play softball because there is too much mud. Tomorrow he will bring his kite. In another week the playground will be dry enough to play ball. Then the children and the teacher will play vigorous games together.

Meadowbrook School was built three years ago. The children study a curriculum similar to that of the nearby public school, but in a different context. In spite of a new building and a young teacher, the methods and materials differ little from those of two generations ago. Even though no science is taught and the third grade does not have a unit on weather, all the children are sensitive to the awakening of nature around them.

The days are getting longer and the amount of pressing farm work is increasing. The children are needed at home to learn the practical art of running a family farm. The teacher is anxious to set her own small garden with vegetable plants and flowers and to get ready for the strawberry harvest. Another school year is drawing to an end, a school year still integrated with the agricultural seasons of planting and harvesting, still related to a family unit in which the school-aged children simultaneously are nurtured by the family and contribute physically to the family's security.

All across America the Old Order Amish children get their formal education in the proverbial "little red schoolhouse" (although in actuality most are painted white). Amish schools have been called "unique, fascinating, puzzling, and immensely successful." The schools are puzzling to moderns because they appear to be quaint remnants of a former era surviving in a high-tech computer age. The schools are strikingly successful in attaining their goals.

Amish rural schools are consistent with farm life of a half-century ago. The teachers are not certified by state standards but are hired for their Christian character, interest in learning, and their ability to deal with children. Most of the teachers are unmarried girls in their early twenties. The schools are true community schools, for they are run and supported by the parents and grandparents. The Amish schools do not teach religious doctrine as do many Protestant church schools. The pupils have no catechism, but together with their teacher they pray the Lord's Prayer and sing hymns. Teachers teach religious values by the example of their lives. Learning to be kind, forgiving, and loving toward one another is understood to be true religion.

On the walls of every school there are posters and pictures, many of them drawn by the pupils or teacher, with moral messages that support cooperative attitudes rather than competitiveness. Absent from the school curriculum are books on science, physical education, computer instruction, and sex education. Also absent are organized sports, clubs, career education, guidance counseling, and television.

School does not separate the Amish child from his brothers and sisters nor does it ignore the value system of his parents. The Amish school child does not feel alienated in school or in a world that is too big for him to comprehend. The Amish have developed a school system that is integrated with their own life, with their family-sized farms and with a rural neighborhood where families help one another.

Although the Amish school is separated from the world outside, it is not separated from Amish life. The school supports the family, the traditions and economy of the Amish community and enables the child to learn both the facts and the roles he needs to function as an Amish person in twentieth-century America. Today the Old Order Amish are quietly developing a school system that is integrated with their own lifestyle; a school system that does not produce alienated youth, but dedicated adults.

Amish parents have served jail terms rather than have their children trained for a way of life not of their choosing. The public school provides preparation for those seeking to participate in mainstream American culture. However, for ethnic and religious groups who think of themselves as "strangers in the land," the expanded role of the public school is threatening. The Old Order Amish are one of several traditional communities who conscientiously reject much of modern technology and new cultural developments. Middle-class values in the public schools threaten a people who want limited isolation from mass communication and protection from the dangers of alienation inherent in the loss of community.

LOCATION AND ORIGIN

The Amish communities are located in the farming regions of the nation. States and Canadian provinces containing Amish schools are shown in Table 1. The total population of the Old Order Amish is estimated to be more than 130,000.

School children enjoy outdoor games at recess time. The black caps on the girls identify a localized conservative group of Amish. (Photo by Fred Wilson.)

With other persecuted German-speaking people, the Amish came to America during the eighteenth century between 1727 and 1790, and during the nineteenth century between 1815 and 1865. They first settled in Berks, Chester, and Lancaster counties in southeastern Pennsylvania. From this location they and the nineteenth-century immigrants from Europe moved westward to other states. The Amish still migrate readily within the United States from one location to another. New communities are constantly being formed while other communities become extinct.

In 1990 there were 784 church districts and a total of 726 schools. Over a ten-year period the number of schools increased from 447 to 726. The Amish have large families. The average number of live births per family is seven. Despite a number of Amish children who do not join the church of their parents, or who leave and become "English" (non-Amish), the Amish rate of population increase is not threatened. In 1990, there were 20,811 pupils enrolled in Amish schools with 976 teachers. The average number of pupils per school is 28.

The location of Amish schools by state is shown in Table 1 and in the frontispiece. Schools are not organized strictly on a congregational level. A school district may encompass two or more congregations. In recently founded Amish settlements such as those in Oklahoma, Texas, and North Carolina, there are new, small schools which are not yet listed in the *Blackboard Bulletin*. Although a Florida congregation exists in winter months, there is no school. The five congregations in Kansas have no Amish schools. Their pupils attend small country public schools. Pennsylvania has 248 schools but 195 churches, while Ohio has 158 schools and 222 churches, and Indiana has 75 schools and 140 church districts. This discrepancy is accounted for by the larger percentage of Amish children who attend public schools in Ohio and Indiana.

The Old Order Mennonites who live in large numbers in Ontario, Pennsylvania, and ten other states are not included in these calculations. They operate 186 schools and have 5,693 pupils.

The Amish are direct descendants of the Swiss Anabaptists of the sixteenth century. The Anabaptists originated in a number of areas simultaneously: the Mennonites arose in Holland and North Germany, the Hutterian Brethren in Moravia, and the Swiss Brethren in Switzerland, all of whom emerged between 1525 and 1536 as forerunners of the "free church" movement (Littell 1964).

All of these groups suffered martyrdom for their deviation from the established state-approved churches, whether Catholic, Lutheran, or Calvinist. Based on their interpretation of the Bible, the Anabaptists held that membership in the Christian church should be voluntary, initiated by adult rather than infant baptism, that the church should be separate from the state, and that Christian believers should practice the teaching and example of Jesus in a disciplined and separated community. Emphasis was placed on simple rather than ostentatious living, regeneration of character, and caring and sharing with the poor. They insisted on loving their enemies and would not fight in or support war. Their attempted reforms were greeted with deportation and death. Many were burned at the stake or were tortured in other cruel ways.

The Amish originated in 1693, establishing themselves 168 years after the

TABLE 1.   AMISH SCHOOLS AND CHURCH DISTRICTS

State or Province	Schools 1980	Schools 1990	Church districts 1990
Ohio	97	153	222
Pennsylvania	146	248	195
Indiana	58	75	140
Wisconsin	26	45	35
Michigan	12	32	32
Missouri	26	34	29
New York	15	28	24
Iowa	20	25	22
Illinois	6	12	18
Ontario (province)	18	20	17
Kentucky	3	14	10
Delaware	6	10	8
Minnesota	8	12	8
Maryland	4	6	6
Tennessee	7	10	6
Kansas	0	0	5
Oklahoma	0	1	3
Florida	0	0	1
Montana	1	1	1
North Carolina	0	0	1
Texas	0	0	1
Total	447	726	784

beginning of the Anabaptist movement as an orthodox branch of the Swiss Brethren (who by this time were also called Mennonites). Elder Jacob Ammann, after whom the Amish were named, differed from the parental Swiss group by emphasizing strict conformity in social and ritualistic practices within a closed community. He advocated the practice of shunning apostate members, insisted on ceremonial footwashing, and simple patterns of grooming and dress styles. Men, for example, were to wear beards. Ostentatious styles (including buttons) of the worldly and wealthy people were to be avoided.

Today there are no Amish in Europe who have retained the name and practices of the original group. Their descendants in Europe have reunited with the main body of Mennonites or have otherwise lost their Amish identity. It is only in North America that the name and the distinctive practices of the Amish have survived.

The name given to the followers in Europe was *Amish-Mennonite* or *Amish*. The name *"Old Order" Amish* came into common usage in nineteenth-century America to distinguish them from the "Progressive" or assimilating groups of Amish. Since the Old Order Amish assemble in private homes for worship, they are sometimes called *House Amish* to distinguish them from the *Church Amish* who worship in meetinghouses. The persistence of custom and a slowness to modernize have been distinctive features of the Old Order. Their communities have remained relatively stable while the dominant culture around them has changed radically.

COMMUNITY ORGANIZATION

In America the Amish people developed a unique community structure. Although their communities are located in various rural regions, they do not typically live in villages, nor do they live in compounds, communes, or in monastic orders. Amish families reside on either side of a highway, around small towns or villages, and are neighbors to "English" (non-Amish) farm families. At the same time they constitute a corporate group in religious and spiritual matters. Dispersed as they are in many states, they try to represent a community of "one mind," "one discipline," and "one body." They attempt to be "in the world, but not of the world" (John 17:16).

Amish community organization has at least four social and spatial components: the *family household, church district, settlement,* and *affiliation.*

The *family household* typically consists of a married couple and their offspring. A farm may have two or even three houses to accommodate the extended family. Family farms are independently owned and are not property of the church.

The *settlement* consists of Amish families living in a contiguous relationship, that is, households that are in proximity. A settlement may be small, consisting of a few households, or it may embrace several counties. The largest settlement is located in Holmes and adjoining counties in Ohio. Next in size is Lancaster County and its vicinity in Pennsylvania. Elkhart and Lagrange counties in Indiana constitute the third largest settlements in America.

A *church district* is a congregation. It has specific geographic boundaries and an ordained leadership. Within the church district worship, baptism, communion, marriage and funerals take place. The size of the district may vary from a few

Family, school, and community are highly integrated in Amish communities. (Lancaster New Era, photo by Martin Heisey.)

families to as many as forty. The boundaries are agreed upon by the leaders and members. When a district becomes too large for the household to accommodate the rotating worship service, it is divided in two. Most families have relatives in nearby or other church districts. There are frequent visits between relatives and friends, but each family has a specific "home church" which is the center of decision-making, ceremony, and mutual-aid activity.

Each congregation chooses its own leaders: usually one bishop, two preachers, and a deacon. The officials are individuals nominated by members, and are ordained by lot for life. They receive no formal training before or after ordination and serve without financial support from the congregation. Every second Sunday the Amish gather for worship services at a home of one of the member couples. On the "off" Sunday when there is no worship service, the day is observed as a sacred day, a time for reading the Bible, resting, visiting, and refraining from all but the most essential chores.

A *church affiliation* is a group of church districts which have a common discipline and commune together. Different affiliations may arise in a settlement when there are differences between progressive and orthodox-minded Amish. "Old Order" Amish, for example, are distinguished from "New Order." These sub-groupings have their analogues in Protestant denominations. For example, it is not sufficient to identify a person as Baptist; one must specify what kind of Baptist.

The Amish tend to rank affiliations according to their degree of worldliness, and on this basis, they distinguish between "low" and "high" church. A low church is one that is orthodox (least similar to the outside world) while a "high" church is one that has relaxed its discipline to allow such things as tractor-driven farm machinery,

Sunday worship services are held in the homes of members.
(Photo by Richard Reinhold.)

telephones, electricity, or simple black automobiles. Large settlements of Amish in the United States have as many as six or even more affiliations.

An Amish group that does not associate ceremonially with another Amish group will say, "We are not *in fellowship* with them." Being "in fellowship" means there is sufficient agreement in the discipline to permit exchange of visiting preachers and to observe communion together.

The Old Order Amish generally have the following discipline in common: worship services in the homes of the members, use of horse-drawn buggies, use of the Pennsylvania-German dialect, a distinctive plain dress for both men and women. All married men have beards (but no mustaches), their hair must not be "shingled," and must be parted in the center if parted at all. Women may not wear printed cloth, bright colored clothes or short hair. Men must wear hook-and-eyes on their dress coats. Homes may not have a central heating system, telephones, or electricity. Automobiles and tractors with pneumatic tires are not permitted. No formal education beyond the elementary grades is permitted, and high school or college diplomas are forbidden.

CORE VALUES

Every human society maintains ideals and guidelines for the rearing of the young. These guidelines can be constructed by anthropologists, whether a society is literate or nonliterate. The process of socialization, that is, acquiring the appropriate attitudes and skills of a responsible functioning adult, takes place within the confines of a culture or cultures. Thus, in acquiring an understanding of Amish socialization, we must know the cultural context: the ideals, institutions, expectations, and rewards.

In this section we will describe the values underlying Amish culture. Values take into account the verbal as well as the nonverbal aspects of culture, and the group's shared goals and perceptions of themselves, as well as their perceptions of others who are not a part of their society. The "ideal" culture may contrast with the "real" culture as expressed in norms that fall short of the "ideal" behavior.

1. Maintaining a Redemptive Community. Like people everywhere, the Amish are engaged in a social discourse with reality. They ask themselves "What is the meaning of life and existence?" They regard themselves as a Christian body suspended in a tension-field between obedience and disobedience to a Supreme Being, an all-knowing and powerful Creator.

Central to the Amish belief is the Biblical story of Creation—the Garden of Eden, with its many plants, animals, birds, and fishes. Man and woman were made by the Creator and enjoyed a spiritual relationship with God. Through disobedience however, they fell from the favor of God and were not only expelled from the Garden of Eden, but they and their children acquired a sinful (or carnal) nature. Redemption and restoration to an eternal or spiritual nature is made possible by God's provision. That provision, described in the New Testament (John 3:16), is the gift of God's son to a world that is hopelessly lost in spiritual darkness.

The Amish believe they are the recipients of this undeserved gift—they must therefore prove themselves worthy, faithful, grateful and humble. They feel obligated to reciprocate for this gift of redemption by offering in return a corporate "body," a community incarnated with the attributes of godliness. These qualities include: walking in righteousness, sacrificial suffering, obedience, submission, humility, and nonresistance. As a corporate offering, this community must be "without spot or blemish" (Eph. 5:27), existing in a state of brotherly love and union, in a state of readiness, and in constant struggle to be worthy as "a bride for the groom" (Rev. 21:2). The individual is implored to choose humility rather than pride, and love for the believing community rather than love for self.

2. Separation from the World.   Separation exists between those who are obedient and those who are alienated from God. There is, therefore, a continuous tension between the two spheres. The Amish believe that as individuals and as a corporate community they must live separate from the "blind, perverted world," (Phil. 2:15) and to have no relationship with the "unfruitful works of darkness" (Eph. 5:11). They know they are "in the world but not of it" (I Pet. 2:11). Social separation is maintained by community rules allowing only limited participation in wider human affairs. Consumptive spending is carefully guarded by specific rules against luxuries and conveniences. The symbols of the redemptive community are explicit, and even a young child can distinguish community symbols from worldly ones.

Living in a community, separated from the world, is essential to spiritual redemption. Amish sermons repeatedly admonish: "Do not love the world system, or the things that keep it going. If anyone loves the world order it is not the Father's love that is in him" (I John 2:15, Jordan tr.). What must be guarded against is the love of physical comforts, the love of material things, and the lust for power.

Separation is mandated by the Biblical admonitions: "Be not conformed to this world. . . ." (Rom. 12:1) and "Be not unequally yoked together with unbelievers" (II Cor. 6:14). These passages forbid members from marrying non-Amish persons, holding a political office, or entering into a business partnership with an outsider (although members may be employed by an outsider). Contacts with the outside world are carefully monitored in order to avoid a possible conflict of interest. Members are forbidden by the precepts and example of Christ to take part in political conflict, violence, or war. When drafted for military service, young men apply for conscientious objector status, basing their stand on Biblical passages such as "My kingdom is not of this world" (John 18:36). Like the early Anabaptists, the Amish today call themselves "defenseless Christians."

In the face of hostility, the Amish will move to new locations without defending their civil or legal rights. When confronted with school consolidation that makes it impossible to remain separate from the world, they build private schools or migrate to other locations. Although the Amish maintain a degree of separation from the world, they are not highly ethnocentric in their personal relations with non-Amish persons. They accept other persons as they are, without attempting to judge them or convert them to the Amish way of life.

Interpreting the meaning of Christianity as community—a voluntary communion of believers—is a recurring theme in Anabaptism. Much of Protestantism, by contrast, has emphasized individualism. It cost the Amish and their ancestors great sacrifice of blood and torment to establish this concept of the "free church" tradition. During the time of their origin, Catholic, Lutheran, and Reformed churches considered them arrogant, exclusive, and heretical.

Much of the Amish ritual today consists of maintaining the purity and unity of the church community. The disobedient, and those who cause disunity must be disciplined or expelled, for a "blemish" cannot be tolerated in the "bride" offered to God. The "old leaven" must be purged from the group (I Cor. 5:7). Twice each year, the church community celebrates the "Lord's Supper" which is the highest form of commitment or spiritual union. Only members who declare their peace with God and with all the other members of the church district may take part.

3. Voluntary Adult Baptism.   Admittance to the redemptive community is voluntary and symbolized by the vow of baptism. Baptism is not merely a ceremony, for the Amish baptism is a life covenant, never to be broken. Receiving baptism signifies loyalty to God and to the corporate community. The Amish do not baptize by immersion or by going into a stream of water; they follow the tradition of pouring a small quantity of water on the head of the kneeling applicant.

In baptism, the young adult acknowledges Christ as the Son of God, belief in the spiritual sovereignty of the true church of God on earth, the "renunciation of the world, the devil, one's own flesh and blood, and confession of Christ as Lord and Savior." The formal confession is not different from other Christian groups. What is significant is the promise to abide by the *Ordnung* (rules that are binding for life) and the promise "not to depart from the discipline in life or death."

Great emphasis is placed on walking the "straight and narrow way." Although free will is emphasized, for one who has been baptized the choice has been made. In support of their religious beliefs, an Amish preacher once told the court, "We don't go down on our knees for nothing." Applicants are warned not to make a promise they cannot keep. The day prior to baptism the applicants are asked to meet with the ministers, at which time they are given the opportunity to "turn back" if they so desire. The young men are asked to accept the duties of a minister should the lot ever fall on them. No young person can be married in the Amish church without first being baptized.

4. The Maintenance of Community Discipline.   After baptism, the individual is morally committed to keep the rules of the church. This means keeping one's behavior more in line with the *Ordnung* than before. The individual assumes responsibility for building the church, which means taking an active part in supporting the community standards. The Amish community is distinct from other church groups in that most of the rules governing life are not specified in writing. These values and norms can be known only by being a participant. The rules for living tend to form a body of sentiments that are essentially a list of "do's and don't's" within the environment of the small Amish community.

Viewed from the outside, the discipline appears to be a heavy weight of tradition having little relationship to real life, but that is not the case when viewed from the vantage point of the participant. Holding modern technology, such as electricity, the telephone, and the automobile, at a distance could not be accomplished without the full support and loyalty of every member of the community. The world's push for bigger and more efficient farm machines is circumvented by the community's rules, and thus the family and community are shielded from middle-class values. The strong family unit, which trains the young in manual work, farming occupations, and domestic work such as gardening, food processing, and caring for young children, is supported by a shared community discipline. Forces which would erode the community, such as convenience, efficiency, and individual manipulation of power, are carefully regulated by the community discipline.

All Amish members know the rules of their church district. Because most rules are common knowledge, it is usually those questionable or borderline issues that are specified in the *Ordnung*. These rules are reviewed at a special service preceding communion. They must have been unanimously endorsed by the ministers. At the members' meeting following the regular service the rules are presented orally, after which members are asked to give assent. A unanimous expression of peace and goodwill toward every member and assent to the *Ordnung* makes possible the observance of communion. Without consensus the communion service cannot be observed, and it may be delayed for a year or more if unanimity is not achieved.

5. *Excommunication and Shunning (Bann und Meidnung)* are the church community's methods of dealing with obdurate and erring members and of keeping the church pure. The exact method of practicing shunning was the central question in the controversy that caused the Amish to withdraw from the Swiss Brethren. The teaching was intrinsic to the Anabaptist movement from its begin-

Family members work cooperatively to achieve common goals.
(Photo by Richard Reinhold.)

ning. The Anabaptist concept of the church was of a pure church consisting of believers only; persons who violated the discipline were first to be excommunicated, then shunned. This method of dealing with offenders, the Amish say, is taught by Christ (Matt. 18:15–17), and explained by the Apostle Paul (I Cor. 5:11); that members must not keep company with unrepentant members nor eat with them. The passages are interpreted to mean that a person who has broken his vow with God and who will not mend his ways must be expelled from fellowship with believers just as the human body casts off an infectious growth. The practice of shunning among the Swiss Mennonites was to exclude the offender from communion. A more emphatic practice was advanced by Jacob Amman. His interpretation required shunning excommunicated persons not only in the communion service but also in social and domestic relationships. Shunning means that members may receive no favors from an excommunicated person, that they may not buy from or sell to an excommunicated person, and that no member shall eat at the same table with an excommunicated person. If the person under the ban is a husband or wife, the couple is to suspend their marital relations until the erring member is restored to the church fellowship. One's obligation to God as represented by the community supercedes one's obligations to the family.

The Amish do not emphasize the evangelism of outsiders. They are not as concerned about the redemption of the outside society as they are about the preservation of their own. They will accept outsiders provided they conform to Amish beliefs and practices. Their primary concern is to keep their own members from "slipping" into the outer world or into other religious groups. Members who wish to have automobiles, radios, or the usual comforts of modern living face the threat of being excommunicated. Thus the ban is used as an instrument of discipline not only for the drunkard or the adulterer, but also for the person who transgresses the discipline of the church. Parents, for example, who send their children to a school beyond that required for living in the Amish community are liable for censure. The same applies to any member who obtains a worldly education.

6. A Life in Harmony with the Soil and Nature.   Implicit in Amish culture is the view that nature is a garden, that man was made to be a caretaker (not an exploiter) in the garden, and that manual labor is good. The material world is viewed as good and not in itself corrupting or evil. The beauty in the universe is perceived in the orderliness of the seasons, the grandeur of the heavens, the intricate world of growing plants, the diversity of animals, and the forces of living and dying. Amish mores require members to make their livelihood from farming or such closely associated activities as carpentry, mason work, or operating a sawmill. Working in factories is a growing trend not approved by the more orthodox Amish. In Europe, the Amish lived in rural areas, always in close association with the soil, so that the community was entirely agrarian in character. In America the Amish have found it necessary to make occupational regulations to safeguard their community from the influence of industrialization and individual competition.

The preference for rural living is reflected in attitudes and informal relations for group life, rather than in an explicit dogma. The Amish believe that God is pleased when man works in harmony with nature, the soil, and the weather, and cares for plants and animals. Hard work, thrift, and mutual aid are virtues. The city, by contrast, is viewed by the Amish as the center of leisure, non-productive spending, and often, wickedness. Family life, they contend, is best maintained away from the cities. God created Adam and Eve to "replenish the earth, and subdue it; and have dominion over the fish of the sea, and over the fowl of the air, and over every living thing that moveth upon the earth" (Genesis 1:28). Man's highest place in the universe is to care for the things of creation. One Amishman said, "The Lord told Adam to replenish the earth and to rule over the animals and the land—you can't do that in cities."

Lancaster County, Pennsylvania, which is a center of Amish life, has long been described as the "garden spot" of the nation, illustrating an intensive method of farming on relatively small holdings. The older residents in Amish communities have accumulated a large amount of agricultural experience and lore reaching back to early colonial days. As farms are handed down from parents to child, so are the experiences and the wisdom associated with the care of livestock and farming. The farm economy incorporates the elements of hard work, cooperative family labor, crop and livestock productivity, and extreme thrift.

These cultural themes play an important part in the education of their children. The Amish are not a part of the mainstream of American culture. Their isolated, intransigent, and withdrawn character has led social scientists to classify them as a sect rather than a denomination. Their negative relation to the larger society enables them to provide for their members a sanctuary from competing value systems. In the face of modern mobility, restlessness, rootlessness, and anxiety, the Amish protect their members against value systems of middle-class society. Worldly success and worldly standards are a threat to the sectarian society, for as sociologists have pointed out, many groups which began as sects (such as Baptists, Methodists, and Congregationalists) have, with the acquisition of wealth, become established denominations. Separation is therefore of utmost importance to the Amish way of life.

If we are to understand the goals of Amish education we must fully appreciate the central concept of separation and its manifestations. In order to survive in an industrialized nation like the United States, most sects have had to retreat to a spatial and psychic togetherness. As geographic isolation becomes less possible with every new invention, interpersonal relations and cohesion within the community become more and more essential for the successful functioning of the sectarian community.

THE GOALS OF EDUCATION: "HUMILITY AND SIMPLE LIVING"

Growing up in a separated society is different from growing up in a mainstream denomination in the United States. In a denomination much of the larger society is affirmed and public education may differ little from the culture of established religions. However, if the Amish child is removed from his community and put into the consolidated school in the large society, there is sharp discontinuity for him. In the Amish school such arbitrary distinctions between school and life do not exist, for the primary function of the Amish school is not education in the narrow sense of instruction, but the creation of a learning environment continuous with Amish

Amish countryside during harvest time. (Photo by Richard Reinhold.)

culture. By identifying with teachers who identify with them, children acquire understanding essential to becoming an adult. The Amish school atmosphere supports the values and attitudes of the separated community, and the individual is socialized to develop his skills and personality within the small community. Emphasis is on interaction and continuity of lives: of teachers, of parents, of pupils, of co-religionists.

The word "education" as used in American society is regarded with suspicion by most Amish people. For them, it signifies ego-advancement, independence, acquisition of power over others, and jeopardy of community life. True education, according to the Amish, is "the cultivation of humility, simple living, and resignation to the will of God." For generations, the group has centered its instruction in reading, writing, arithmetic, and the moral teachings of the Bible. They stress training for life participation (here and for eternity) and warn of the perils of "pagan" philosophy and the intellectual enterprises of "fallen man," as did their forefathers. Historically, the Anabaptists avoided all training associated with self-exaltation, pride of position, enjoyment of power, and the arts of war and violence. Memorization, recitation, and personal relationships between teacher and pupil are part of a system of education that is supremely social and communal.

The following postulates, derived from examination of historical sources and verified by observations, express the Amish view not only of formal education, but also of human nature and the ultimate goals of training the young.

BELIEFS ABOUT HUMAN NATURE

1. Although children are believed to have inherited a sinful nature through no fault of their own, they are considered loving and teachable, and with the proper

environment, by the time they become adults, are capable of assuming responsibility to God and man for their actions.

2. Parents are responsible for training their children and are morally accountable to God for teaching them right from wrong and giving them a knowledge of eternal life.

3. Children are urged not to be idle but to learn to read and write so that they may acquire a knowledge of the scriptures. Learning manual skills that are useful for making a living is also encouraged.

4. Obedience to parents, and ultimately to God, is a cardinal virtue. Children are not to be self-willed, but well-mannered, quiet, and humble in the presence of others.

5. The family and, to a lesser extent, the school are believed to have the primary responsibility for training the child for life. Limited individualism within the bounds of faithful adult behavior is the model for the child. It is believed that the child must have an explicit relationship to his parents, siblings, church, community, and school to achieve adequate training for adult life.

6. The school is viewed as an instrument for teaching children the literacy and skills needed to live as productive adults in an environment where values taught in the home are continuous and function throughout the life cycle. The home and the church, rather than the school, are responsible for the religious training of the young.

7. Children during their age of innocence are regarded as pure and not in need of ceremonial baptism. Should they die in their innocence, original sin is not

Amish school children are engaged in meaningful farm work.
(Photo by Richard Reinhold.)

imputed to them, on account of the death of Christ. Their entrance into adult-hood and the church-community is attained through familiarity with the scrip-tures, followed by faith and baptism after attaining adulthood.

8. Acceptance of mature social responsibility involves total commitment to the believing church community and material and spiritual separation from worldly standards. This includes association and marriage only with members of the believing community, and a personal willingness to suffer persecution or death in order to maintain the faith.

Total separation is not a goal, nor do the Amish think of themselves as better than other people. Wholeness and separation are not considered antithetical, but complementary with the continued existence of a prized way of life. Like parents in any society, the Amish want their children to absorb the basic values of their way of life. Many Amish fear the loss of their cohesive spiritual tradition. Their concern is not simply that their children may become "English," but that they may be spiritually lost for eternity. Inability to teach their children the Amish way of life affects the parents' relation to God, the community, and themselves. Parents are accountable to God for rearing their children in the faith and to fail to do this is to leave a blemish on the church. To lose one's children to the world is to lose hope of spending eternity with them in heaven.

METHODS OF THE STUDY

Implicit in our approach is the assumption that every culture provides guidelines for the rearing of the young and that these guidelines can be articulated by the anthropologist. Our study is not directly concerned with legal or political questions. It focuses instead on the indigenous processes of nurturing and socialization, as well as on formal schooling in the context of Amish culture. It attempts to illustrate the cultural context of learning—the cultural goals, the institutions, the practices, individual participation in the culture, and pupil achievement—in relation to the whole of Amish society. Where conflict exists between the public school system and Amish schooling, an attempt is made to bring anthropological insights to bear on the problem.

Our study deals with the Old Order Amish as distinguished from several more assimilated groups of Amish—the Amish Mennonites, Church Amish, or New Order Amish—who have altered their lifestyles by owning automobiles, using electricity and telephones in their homes, and showing greater readiness to verbalize their personal religious experience. The whole of Old Order Amish culture is illustrated in this study insofar as it relates to socialization. For more extensive treatment of Amish ethnography, the reader should consult the bibliography found at the end of this book.

The scope of our field studies included Amish communities in Pennsylvania, Ohio, Indiana, and several other states with smaller settlements. Socialization practices from infancy through old age were observed while residing in farm communities. As participant observers, the fieldworkers were identified with a specific family, its network of kinship and visiting patterns, ceremonial functions, and the daily routine of farm and community activities. Interviews were informal and unstructured, but data were systematically obtained and recorded. Repeat visits to the community and shorter visits to other communities with Amish members were important means of obtaining longitudinal data on human growth and community changes. Observations were conducted in Amish schools, in public schools with Amish enrollments, and in a control group consisting of a modern rural school.

2 / Socialization Patterns and the Life Cycle

Age stages differ from one society to another, but at least seven age/sex categories are universally recognized. The Amish recognize six age categories, with several less well-defined stages within their culture. The stages in the Amish life cycle are not as sharply delineated as in many cultures, and although each stage tends to correspond to a biological phase, the social functions of each group are culturally determined. Some knowledge of the age structure of Amish society is essential to understanding Amish socialization patterns from birth to death.

THE AGE STAGES

In Amish society a person passes through a series of six distinct age categories or stages of socialization as one progresses through life. Different behavior is demanded at each stage. The stages, from birth to death, are as follows:

Babies.   This first stage covers the period from birth until the child walks. Children of this age are generally referred to as "babies."

Little Children.   The second stage covers the period between walking and entrance into school, generally at the age of six or seven. Sometimes they are spoken of as "children at home," although that phrase more often refers to all children who are unmarried and still eat and sleep under the parental roof.

Scholars.   Children attending school are referred to as "scholars" by the Amish. These children are fulfilling the eight years of elementary schooling required by the state. They attend either public schools or Amish schools and are between the ages of six and fifteen.

Young People.   Young people (or "youth") are those who have completed eight years of schooling and can therefore do a full day's work. Young people participate in the social life of their peers as distinct from the family-centered social activity that characterizes the other age stages in Amish culture. "Young people" are those persons between the ages of about fifteen and marriage (marriage takes place in the early twenties.) There are several subdivisions within this age stage. Those young people who have finished elementary school but are not yet fifteen are generally not full participants in the social life of this group. Those young people who have been baptized are, in many communities, no longer full participants in this age group either, for they have voluntarily chosen to abide by the rules of the church and are no longer testing the boundaries of their culture. The military draft,

19

which had previously removed Amish young men from the community for two years of alternative service, was never integrated into the age patterning of Amish culture.

Adulthood.   Baptism signifies religious adulthood, but marriage and the birth of the first child brings social maturity. Generally the time interval between baptism and marriage is relatively short. The major activity during adulthood is childrearing.

Old Folks.   Adults generally retire sometime after their youngest child has married and started to raise a family. The old couple moves from the big house into the "grandfather house" or to the edge of the village. They are cared for by their children and exert a conservative influence as they fulfill their accepted role of admonishing the young.

ADULTHOOD

Age grading in Amish society must begin with a discussion of adults, for the family is the basic unit of Amish culture. The most important family activity is childrearing. Household size may vary from those married pairs who have no children to those who have 14 or more children. Studies of family size show that for completed families the average number of children is seven. If an Amish leader is asked how big his church district is, he will answer with the number of families, not with the number of individuals. An Amish schoolteacher will tell you how many families attend the school, and when the teacher introduces the children, he or she will often introduce them by family rather than by grade.

The Amish family is marked by its stability. Theologically, the Amish believe that the commitment to one's spouse is second only to the commitment to God. Husband and wife become one flesh, a single unit separable only by God. The question of sacrificing family for profession never comes up. The family comes first. A job is of no intrinsic importance; it is necessary because it supplies the economic basis for the family. The work of the household should provide vocational education for the children and fulfill the biblical standard, "In the sweat of thy face shalt thou eat bread" (Gen. 3:19). Although the Amish family is patriarchal and the husband is the head of the wife, the wife has an immortal soul and is therefore not merely an extension of her husband, nor wholly subservient to him. Her relative position is illustrated by her position in church, where she has an equal vote but not an equal voice.

Parents are expected to serve as examples for the child. An Amish minister admonishes, "Our lives should, by all means, be separated from the world, and be so consecrated, that our children can see by our words and deeds. . . ." Parents do not have individual rights; they have responsibilities and obligations for the correct nurture of their children. An Amishman says, "I am a father. . . . I must teach, train, admonish, chasten, love, and guide my children, and all this with patience and wisdom." In his final admonition before his death, an Amish preacher wrote to his sons, "The responsibility to teach your children lies fully upon you [parents]." Parents are believed to be accountable to God for their children's spiritual welfare. The Amish quote Menno Simons, the sixteenth-century founder of the Mennonites, who said, "Watch over their [your children's] souls as long as they are under your care, lest you lose also your own salvation on their account."

Amish parents act as a single unit when dealing with their children and reinforce one another. Referring to repeated misbehavior of one of her children, an Amish woman said, "We finally decided we would have to spank him if he did it again. He was late again so Amos took him into the bedroom to spank him. I went too because I should help by being there. The boy must know that both of us are concerned." Admonitions to parents in the sermons and in Amish writings are directed not to fathers as such or to mothers alone, but to parents. Parents are taught that if there is a difference of opinion between them, they should discuss it privately and prayerfully and always be of one mind when disciplining the child. The wife is expected to support her husband in all things, especially in his relationship with other people, whether it be their children, a parent, or friends and neighbors. The husband in turn should be considerate of his wife on a physical, emotional, and spiritual level. The ideal is to be individuals to one another, but of one mind to all others.

Amish parents are remarkably consistent in the demands they make on their children and in the behavior they expect of them. They constantly reinforce one another and there is general consensus within the community as to how children ought to be raised and how they ought to behave at different stages.

Children function as socializing agents for their parents in a variety of ways. As parents strive to be good examples for their children, they modify their own behavior. In their efforts to teach their children to become good Amish persons, they become better Amish themselves. The birth of a child enhances the status of the parents within the community. With parenthood they attain full adulthood. Children take up so much time and energy that the parents are not likely to have time for other interests. Today, because most doctors refuse to come to the house and midwives may be unavailable, many Amish babies are born in the hospital. Medically this may be advantageous, but culturally it is not. Home births have a positive value in uniting the family. They demonstrate the wife's unique, dramatic contribution and strengthen her position in the patriarchal family. The husband and wife grow closer by sharing the experience of childbirth. Where available, many Amish take advantage of natural childbirth programs so that the father can remain with the mother during labor and childbirth. Amish women do not see childbirth as threatening, but as status-enhancing. The most traditional Amish have continued to oppose hospital deliveries and with the help of sympathetic doctors or midwives some of them still quietly give birth at home (Armstrong 1986). Birth control is not practiced among the conservative Amish.

BABIES

Babyhood is the stage between birth and walking. The Amish believe a baby is a pleasure. The newborn may be enjoyed without fear of self-pride, for the baby is a gift from God and not primarily an extension of the parents. At this tender age a baby can do no wrong. If he cries, he is in need of comfort, not discipline. It is believed that a baby can be spoiled by wrong handling, especially by nervous, tense handling, but the resultant irritability is the fault of the environment, not the baby; he remains blameless. An Amish baby is born into the community. A baby is never spoken of as "a little stranger," but is welcomed as a "new woodchopper" or a "little dishwasher." Future sex roles are recognized, but there is little difference in the care given a boy or girl. Each baby is greeted happily as a contribution to the security of the family and the church.

Amish babies are rarely alone. They sleep in their parents' room, are moved around the house during the day, and in a large family are held during most of their waking hours. They are diapered and bathed on their mother's lap, not on a hard, cold table or tub; it is a time of happy sociability. Babies are rarely fed on a strict time schedule, but in relation to their own pattern of hunger and the work pattern of the family. Solid food is given at the family table during family meals. The family attitude is one of sharing its good food with the baby. Babies as young as five or six months are believed not to eat well if fed alone. It is generally thought that everyone eats better in a group; eating is an important social activity. When parents are visiting, at church, traveling, or ill, friends and members of the extended family help with one another's babies. During the first year of life the baby receives solicitous care from a large number of Amish of all ages.

The relaxed handling of babies within the home or the community is quite different from the care taken of them when mother and baby make an excursion into the world. The baby is tightly wrapped and covered, often hidden in his mother's shawl. The face may be covered in order to protect the baby from the "bad air." Passing strangers would probably not realize that the mother was carrying a baby. The traditional Amish dislike having their babies cared for by outsiders or even noticed by them. The way the baby is handled when the mother is shopping or traveling shows the Amish distrust of the outside world and the parents' efforts to protect the baby from its malevolent influence. Old Order Amish parents give generous attention to their babies' needs, both physical and social. This care equips the baby to trust persons. Babies are enjoyed by the Amish; they are believed to be gentle, responsive, and secure within the home and the Amish community, but vulnerable when out in the world. Babies are held, talked to, and directed. They are not scolded or punished, and there is no such thing as a bad baby, although there may be a difficult baby.

LITTLE CHILDREN

The little child or preschool stage lasts from walking until entrance into elementary school. During the preschool years a child is taught to respect and obey those in authority, to care for those younger and less able than he, to share with others and to help others, to do what he is taught is right and to avoid that which is wrong, to enjoy work, and to fulfill his work responsibilities pleasantly. The parents' task in these years is to create a safe environment for their children. The parents live separated from the world, maintaining the boundary for their children and striving always to protect them from both physical and moral danger.

The children are taught to respect authority, and respect is shown by obedience. The Amish do not strive for blind obedience, but for obedience based on love and on the belief that those in authority have deep concern for one's welfare and know what is best. Children learn this relationship between authority and responsibility very early. The four-year-old child is expected to hand over his toy to the three-year-old if the three-year-old cries for it, but in the parents' absence the three-year-old should do what the four-year-old tells him to. However, the older child may not make arbitrary demands of the younger, and he is expected to cajole rather than force the younger child into cooperation. The children learn in this way that authority must be obeyed. Those in authority do not simply give orders; they also nurture and protect those under their authority.

Most traditional Amish parents teach obedience by being firm and consistent, rather than by violent confrontations or single instances of breaking the child's will. The switch is used freely, but not harshly. In their handling of disobedience, Amish parents vary somewhat in the age at which obedience is deemed necessary, the degree of obedience demanded, the length to which parents will go to obtain obedience, and their emotional attitude in handling the disobedient child. None of the Amish condone wilfulness, stubbornness, or defiance on the part of the child, but they may have different opinions as to whether a child's behavior is caused by stubbornness or lack of understanding. The traditional Amish are matter-of-fact rather than moralistic in dealing with their children. The Amish believe that children naturally want to be helpful.

Work is perceived as helping others and fulfilling one's responsibility to them. A child is rarely thanked for doing his chores. Thanks are not expected for carrying out responsibilities. More often the parent may make a simple statement, "Now the floor is clean." The child is rewarded by the task having been accomplished. Work well done is its own reward. Children are trained to help one another rather than to be independent. Thus a four-year-old child will get the boots for the two-year-old and put them on for him, then instead of putting on his own boots he will wait for his older sister to help him. Although the Amish girls always wear dresses and the little boys, after they are toilet-trained, wear trousers, there is little difference in tasks they are taught to perform. Boys are encouraged to like horses and machinery, but children of both sexes accompany their father around the farm and help their mother with simple household tasks.

Young preschool children may scream to get attention or to solicit adult protection from teasing by another child or from the aggression of an age-mate. This is not acceptable for an older child, who is expected to be able to cope with the situation without summoning adult help. Anyone is permitted to cry in response to deep emotion, but tears are discouraged as a response to physical pain or self-pity.

Amish preschool children have great freedom of movement as they accompany their father around the farm, care for a younger sibling, or run simple errands for their mother or grandmother. They are encouraged to be useful but are not pushed to tasks beyond their ability. The environment is neither harsh nor over-protective. Initiative in the physical realm is encouraged, but intellectual initiative or asking questions is severely channeled. The Amish child develops the feeling that his physical participation in the world of adults is good, but that his questions are often a nuisance or foolish. He acquires a sense of caution about initiating new ideas. Instead of asking how or why, he learns to observe and imitate on a behavioral level.

The presence of the father in and around the home is considered necessary for the proper upbringing of preschool children. As more Amish fathers work in specialized jobs such as carpentry that take them away from the home for part of each day, there is some concern expressed that the children cannot be properly taught.

The family, church, and community have an essential role to play in the socialization of the preschool child. Preschool children attend church with their parents; they sit through the long service—the girls usually with their mothers, the boys often with their fathers—learning to be considerate of others, quiet, and patient. After the service they share in the community meal and perhaps take a nap on a big bed with other Amish babies. The rest of the time they play freely and vigorously about the house and yard, safe in the presence of many adults who care for them and guide them. If a small child suddenly feels lost, someone quickly returns him to a member of his family. To the preschooler the community seems to be composed of many people, all of whom know him and protect him. He is comfortable and secure within the encompassing community.

Preschool Amish children are kept as far away from the outside world as is practical. When shopping with their parents, they stay very close to them. Little Amish children are not introduced to non-Amish and are not taught about the world outside the community. They may know the exact location of many farms, but not the road to the nearest city.

The Amish do not send their children to kindergarten. Their policy states: "Kindergarten is not sanctioned by the Amish people. Children of this age should be under parents' care. The nurture and admonition that Moses received while under the care of his mother was implanted so deep, that after being taught the wisdom of the Egyptians, [he] chose rather 'to suffer affliction with the people of God, than to enjoy the pleasure of sin for a season' " (*Guidelines,* p. 22). In some communities children who will be first-graders in the Amish school the following autumn will visit school in the spring to become acquainted with the new surroundings.

SCHOLARS

The children in this stage, between the ages of about 6 and 15 years, are called scholars. Throughout the school years the family continues to be the primary locus for the child's socialization. Amish families continue to teach their school-age children the same attitudes and values they taught to their preschoolers, and they maintain much the same relation to them in respect to the community and the world. The parents' role is protective and supportive as well as didactic. The parent has the responsibility to punish transgressions, but also the power to forgive. Punishment is used primarily as necessary for the safety of the child: for his physical safety ("stay away from that nervous horse"), for his cultural safety ("be respectful to older people"), for his legal safety ("don't fish without a fishing license"), or for his moral safety ("be obedient"). Rewards are used to develop the right attitudes in the child: humility, forgiveness, admission of error, sympathy, responsibility, and appreciation of work. Children are motivated primarily by concern for other people and not by fear of punishment.

The Amish emphasize that children are the responsibility of their parents. The school and the church are supplemental. The parents must see that their children stay within the discipline of the church. If they do not, the preacher or deacon should talk to the parents, not to the children, about their laxness. The school's task is to cooperate with the parent to preserve the faith taught by the parents, for it is the role of the family, not of the school or even the church, to make Christians of the children.

The parents of school-age children are not only teaching their children Christianity, they are also teaching them the work skills necessary to live an Amish Christianity. By the time the child is eight or nine he begins to have fairly demanding tasks to perform. Boys tend to help their fathers and girls work with their mothers. But everyone helps, regardless of sex, where he is most needed. Formerly the Amish felt secure enough about their children of six or seven, to hand them over to the world for their schooling. During the last 35 years, however, changes in the public schools and in the surrounding rural American culture have created greater problems for the Amish. Modern consolidated schools are not suitable agents of socialization for the Amish child. Two reactions to the disruptive influence of the public school are possible, both of which are currently being tried. The first is to tolerate the public school, attempting to isolate its influence and to counteract the disruption it causes. The second solution is for the Amish to build and conduct their own schools, a new undertaking for the Amish community which has become the preferred solution.

The primary function of the Amish school is to teach Amish children the three R's in an environment where they do not have to learn the assumptions of twentieth-century America, where they can learn discipline, true values, and getting along with each other in life. Participants in a county Amish school meeting reported that "our goal should be that the church, the home, and the school should teach the same things. Let us not confuse our children, but help them to fill their places in the church and community." By contrast the public schools train children to function as individuals, to make their place in the world, and to find a community of their choosing.

Amish elementary pupils generally have similar experiences within their families and within the community, but their contact with the world differs greatly, depending on whether they attend a public school or an Amish school. Over-simplifying somewhat for purposes of illustration, we will contrast the two types of schools as socializing agents for the Amish school-age child. A primary difference between the public and the Amish school is its relation to the community. The public school is a part of the outside world and the Amish feel that they have little hope of affecting it. Amish parents, therefore, participate minimally in the public schools. The Amish build their own schools, not only with their own money, but also with their own hands. They make all the decisions, within the limits of the state

Children are introduced to manual skills early in life.
(Photo by Richard Reinhold.)

law, about the school calendar, the subjects to be taught, the teachers to be hired, and the books to be used. Parents, ministers, and travelers from other Amish communities are always welcome visitors at the school. Physically and emotionally the school belongs within the Amish community.

Operating private schools introduces certain problems within the Amish community. Supporting an Amish school is sometimes an economic strain. A certain amount of borrowing of techniques and practices from worldly schools is necessary. Therefore, unless carefully managed, the boundary between the world and the church may become blurred. This is especially true if the community is not "of one mind." Misunderstandings sometimes arise because the roles of the teacher and the school board members are still becoming formalized. Regional and national meetings, attended by teachers, board members, and ministers, help define the teacher's role within both the school and the larger Amish community. Some Amish parents are concerned that the children learn too little about the world when they attend only Amish schools. The Amish realize that one must understand the world fairly well in order to reject it selectively and in such a way that survival is possible within the twentieth century. They feel that Amish children should master English and understand the ways of worldly people to the extent that is necessary for business transactions with them.

Both the public schools and the Amish schools teach the three R's, but their methods are quite different and their attitudes toward the ultimate use of the knowledge is very different. The public schools use a greater variety of material and they stress speed, sometimes at the expense of accuracy. The Amish schools tend to use a more limited amount of material, but the children learn it thoroughly. They stress accuracy rather than speed, drill rather than variety, proper sequence rather than freedom of choice. The public school tends to teach subject matter as a tool needed by the child to achieve social mobility and to realize the highest individual potential. The Amish schools teach the same material, but they aim to help the child become a part of the community and remain within the community. They emphasize shared knowledge rather than individualized knowledge and the dignity of tradition rather than progress.

In public schools, children are separated from their siblings and placed into narrow age groups. Individual achievement is emphasized. In Amish schools brothers and sisters are in the same room, age-grading is not so rigid, and group excellence or group competition is used as a stimulus. A whole school will strive to have a perfect score in spelling; a chart will be kept of each class's average in the arithmetic test scores. This method is similar to the use of competition in the Soviet children's collectives, where competition is used to enhance the group and build group responsibility rather than to bring praise to the individual.

Public schools tend to teach that weakness is bad and should be overcome by the individual; Amish schools assume that all individuals are weak and that they need help from one another and from a higher power as well as individual effort in order to improve. Within the public school the child is regarded as a citizen and an intellect; within the Amish school, as a future Amishman and a soul. In the public school a teacher's academic training, knowledge of his subject, and teaching techniques are the criteria for hiring. In the Amish school the teacher's example in daily life and wisdom are more important than training and factual knowledge. Amish teachers have no tenure, for obviously someone who turns out to be a poor teacher is not fulfilling the role God intended for him and should do some other, more suitable kind of work. Public elementary school is conceived as preparing the child for high school, not as sufficient in itself. The Amish school assumes that the child will go on learning for the rest of his life, but that his formal schooling will end with the eighth grade.

The dangers of public school for Amish children are not only the differences in attitudes between their parents and their teacher, not only the specific subject matter taught in the public school, not only such frills as visual aids and physical education, but also the possibility that the children may form close personal friendships with non-Amish children and become too comfortable in the ways of the world. Continuity with faith, family, and community would then be broken.

During their school years the Amish children spend most of their time outside of school at home with their family or visiting the homes of friends and relatives with their family. The family attends church as a unit, and people of all ages listen to the same service. The Amish schoolchildren, unlike the typical suburban schoolchild, are usually in a mixed age group rather than isolated with their peers (Bronfenbrenner 1970:96–102, 115). The Amish child who attends an Amish school shares the classroom with seven other grades. These children know many adults in addition to the parents, and the adults have a comfortable interest in each child's development.

During the elementary school years Amish children are encouraged in their efforts to make things with their own hands. Girls cook, bake, sew, and make things for their family. Boys often build toys or birdhouses, and they help with the farmwork, learning the necessary routine of feeding poultry and livestock. Their

All ages enjoy the work and sociability of a barn raising. The women watch the construction but they also cook and serve a full meal to the work crews.
(Photo by Fred Wilson.)

The men are carying a pre-cut wooden beam for the barn's structure.
(Photo by Richard Reinhold.)

These boys play barn raising with the scraps of lumber. (Photo by Fred Wilson.)

sense of industry is enhanced by the work of their hands, by being praised and rewarded with the results, and by being allowed to finish their products. The child in an Amish school never sees television. The home and the family, real people, not two-dimensional characters, play a central role in the life of the Amish school child whose source of industry depends to a great extent on all the adults in his life—not only the teacher. His real world includes the home and family, which play a central role in development. The school child has many role models and many informal teachers.

YOUNG PEOPLE

Young people are those in the age category from about 16 years old until marriage. In this stage the Amish individual progresses toward adulthood in an orderly, clearly defined manner through a series of accepted stages. Two governmental institutions, schooling and the military draft may threaten this order by prolonging childhood in one case and adolescence in the other. Forcing an Amish person to attend school daily places the individual in the child category, for the hours spent in school prevent the child from doing a full day's work, which is the criterion for achieving the status of young adult. The alternative service program of the draft removed the young man from the community and from the opportunity to accept an adult role, thereby extending his adolescence. When the individual is prevented by the state from achieving a status position within his culture believed to be his due, both the individual and the culture suffer.

Compulsory schooling appeared with the growth of the industrialized state and is tied to industry, government, and the military. In the United States, school is a prerequisite for membership in a managerial middle class. The Amish reject membership in a managerial middle class; they reject urbanization, industrialization, and participation in the armed services, and they reject the training that would prepare them for unacceptable occupations. They withdraw their children at the end of elementary school—or in some areas at the end of vocational school—to train them within the home and the community to become skilled in and to enjoy the work they will actually be doing as adults.

The Amish have consistently maintained that further formal education beyond elementary school is not only unnecessary but detrimental to the successful performance of Amish adult work roles. Studies seem to verify these assumptions, suggesting, for example, that the over-educated are less productive, whether they are factory workers or elementary school teachers, and that in many kinds of work, on-the-job training is more important than educational credentials. Certainly the skills the Amish need are best learned by doing. The enjoyment of physical labor can be learned better by laboring than by studying in a classroom.

For an individual to become Amish the person must be kept within the Amish community, physically and emotionally, during the crucial adolescent years. High school removes the Amish young person from the community by changing his or her status, by physically removing the child from the farm and the house, by teaching the young person skills and attitudes that are disruptive to the Amish way of life, and by enabling the individual to form personal friendships with non-Amish students. The school is disruptive both in what it teaches the Amish child and in what it prevents the pupil from learning. If the Amish boy is in school, he cannot attend sales and learn how to buy and sell in the worldly market. The child cannot attend work bees or weddings or church services on special occasions nor learn the adult roles of social integration. Amish children who attend high school may experience conflict and anguish that carry into adulthood.

In this age stage excursions will be made out into the world, but, it is hoped, not until late in adolescence. Nor should these excursions last for long. They should never remove the young person to a great physical distance from an Amish community. Amish young people may work for "English people," in this way learning about the world, but they must return home every weekend. Young people may work in small rural factories, but they return home in the evening and do not join labor unions. Even this amount of contact with the world is usually not permitted until almost the end of this age stage. If it appears that the young person is not ready for this degree of contact, his or her parents may try to make the person quit his worldly work.

During adolescence the peer group is of supreme importance, for most of the Amish young person's socialization takes place within this group rather than within the church or the family. If the young person's peer group remains Amish, that person has a reference point, a balance, and a support. Even though as an individual or as a member of the Amish peer group, he or she transgresses many rules and crosses most of the boundaries between the Amish community and the world, that person will eventually return to the church and become a faithful member. However, if during this stage the young person makes English friends and identifies with an alien peer group, even though that person is well-behaved, he or she will probably leave the Amish church never to return.

Courting age, called *rum springa* or "running around," begins at about 16. Attendance at Amish young people's gatherings are important aspects of socialization during this period. The most important gathering is the Sunday evening singing attended by the young people. Aside from hymn singing, it is an evening of informal association, where an hour or more is spent visiting and joking, and where dates are arranged. Other social occasions are at weddings, cornhusking bees, and various kinds of mutual aid parties or "frolics." In addition to taking his girl home on Sunday evenings after the singing, in some communities a young man who is going steady will see his girlfriend every other Saturday evening at her home. When Saturday evening comes, he dresses in his best, and making a quiet departure from his home, he may leave the impression that he is going to town on business. Secrecy pervades the entire period of courtship regardless of its length. Most boys marry between the ages of 22 and 24. Girls on the average tend to be a year younger than boys when marrying.

The choice of a mate is conditioned by the values of Amish culture. A boy must obtain a partner from his own Amish faith, but not necessarily from his own community. Young people intermarry among Amish districts of the same affiliation and among settlements that maintain "fellowship" with one another. Marriage must be endogamous with respect to religious affiliation, for an Amish person who marries a non-Amish person is excommunicated and shunned.

First-cousin marriages are taboo and second-cousin marriages are discouraged, but do occur. The newly married couple receive economic assistance from both of their parents, often consisting of furniture, a cook stove, livestock, and basic farming equipment. Every mother is concerned that each of her children receive a homemade quilt and comforter. These are often made several years in advance so they will be ready when marriage takes place.

Conscription during wartime has been especially disruptive to the Amish. Throughout their history the Amish have been pacifists, refusing to serve in any army. During the Vietnam conflict, drafted Amish young men spent two years performing alternative service under the Selective Service classification of 1-W. This service outside the community was disruptive both to the individual and to the community. As required by law, Amish men register with the military upon reaching age 18, and in the event of conscription they would request conscientious objector status.

Baptism is an important *rite de passage* among the Amish, for it signifies not only total commitment to the believing church-community, physically and spiritually separated from the world, but also signifies admission to adulthood.

Prior to baptism a certain degree of adolescent rebellion may become institutionalized among the youth. The Amish child is raised in a carefully protected environment by relatively authoritarian parents and teachers. However, by the close of this age stage the Amish young person will have made the two greatest commitments of his life: he will have decided to join the church and will have chosen a spouse. He is expected to make these commitments as an individual with the help of God. In order to make such important decisions he must establish a degree of independence from his family and to some extent from his community in order to develop his own identity. This is done in many ways, most of them carefully institutionalized. First, the family relaxes some of its tight control over the young person. He goes to social gatherings of his peers rather than having all of his social life with his family. This is believed to be a time during which the young person learns what it means to be Amish. The community does not officially have control over him. During this period, Amish young people may test some of the boundaries of the Amish community. They may perhaps own a radio, have a photograph taken, attend a movie, or occasionally wear clothes that are outside the *Ordnung*. As long as these forays are discreet, they are ignored by the parents and the community, for it is believed the young person should have some idea of the world he or she is voluntarily rejecting. One of the reasons courtship is secretive is that this is a means of achieving privacy in a closely knit community and within a large family. The young people are protected by a degree of institutionalized "blindness" on the part of adults who thereby give them some freedom.

Earlier in life the Amish child accepted being Amish as part of his or her identity. During this stage the young person strives to determine what it means personally to be Amish. The family and the community help by overseeing vocational training. Both the young Amishman and young Amishwoman work for a variety of different people during these years, learning various acceptable vocational roles and getting, through their jobs, a knowledge of other Amish families and other Amish communities and perhaps a glimpse of the world by working for non-Amish. During their working hours the young people are respectful of community standards. However, during free time with their peers, there is considerable testing of boundaries and striving for self-knowledge. This period is made much more difficult if the young person attends high school, is removed from the community by military conscription, develops close friendships with English young people, or is exposed to a fundamentalist religious group. When any of these things happen, there may be a long and difficult period during which the young person strives towards integration. In the more typical cases, where the Amish young person remains emotionally within the community, there is rarely much role confusion. The typical Amish young person is not an impatient idealist nor in search of a unique identity. The preparation for this phase of life began in the cradle. The child was cared for in such a way that he developed confidence in his physical participation in his environment coupled with some insecurity in the area of manipulating ideas. There is a basic continuity between what Amish young people learn as children and what they experience as adolescents. By the end of this age-stage the Amish adolescent is able to bring together his or her newfound abilities—the things he or she has learned about himself or herself as a person, a family member, a worker, a member of the Amish peer group—and integrate these images of himself or herself into a whole that makes sense. Within the family and community the young person arrives at a sense of who he or she is, where he or she has come from, and where he or she is going.

OLD FOLKS

Amish socialization provides the individual with resources for meeting the major problems of aging: the inactivity of retirement, economic insecurity, prestige loss, social isolation, loss of health, and death. The Amish accept aging realistically as a natural stage of human life. The care of the aged does not depend on a single institution; it is part of the total way of life.

The age of retirement for either men or women in Amish society is not rigidly defined by the culture and varies widely among household heads. If the children are married and in need of farms, the father may decide to retire as early as 50. Where pressure for farms is not a consideration, the head of the family may in rare cases decide not to retire until the age of 70. Retirement is voluntary and often gradual rather than abrupt. Even after retirement, work and activity do not change much, for grandparents usually assist their married children in times of specific need. Health is a factor in determining the onset of retirement. Work expectations can be reduced without fear of losing prestige, and men are not forced to choose between full-time jobs and doing nothing at all. Obligations such as attending funerals and visiting the sick and the bereaved increase with age.

Moving into the "grandfather house" is the normal way of retiring. The old folks move into the adjacent farm dwelling and live from their life savings, which are supplemented by a share in the farm (to which the parents usually maintain title) and a modest income from carpentry or other part-time work as long as health permits. Separate living arrangements and independence of travel are important personal liberties respected by the Amish system of retirement. Grandparents continue to have their own kitchen and own horse and buggy. The Amish do not apply for old age and survivors' insurance benefits. The economic aspects of retirement are not major considerations. What is most important is a mode of life that permits continuity between the generations and associations between grandparents and grandchildren.

Prestige tends to increase with age, so that old age brings no noticeable evidence of anxiety due to loss of status. Older men and women both have a formal vote in the church business sessions. The association of age with respect in a patriarchal society tends to strengthen the ties with the past. Old-fashioned ways are revered and a knowledge of these ways is perpetrated by the older people. Young farmers ask their fathers for advice on a variety of farm management problems. Mothers ask grandmothers for advice on how to rear their children, even though they do not always follow their instructions. Such interaction between the age groups lessens the strain between the generations.

Social life is balanced between privacy and social involvement. Privacy is available for the elderly individual or couple, while participation in the church and community activity continues naturally. In fact, retirement from church offices, such as those of bishop, deacon, or preacher, is not possible since ordination is a lifetime calling. Psychological isolation and loneliness are not major problems. Togetherness is fostered in religious life, kinship and visiting patterns, and agricultural pursuits involving much hand labor allows children and parents to work and live in proximity to each other. The psychological aspects of aging are acknowl-

A typical Ohio Amish homestead. Two houses indicate that a retired couple, the
grandparents or a young couple, live in one of the houses.
(Photo by Fred Wilson.)

edged and are met by the community and the family. The slow rate of change and
strong community ties in Amish society assure older people of ample opportunities
for meaningful social participation to the limit of their physical energy and mental
capacities.

The Old Order Amish people do not build separate institutions or homes for the
aged. The aged are therefore not physically removed from their children and
grandchildren. The firm teaching among the Amish that children should obey their
parents places a moral obligation of reciprocity on the young married people to
provide for their aging parents.

The manner in which the culture influences the psychosocial adjustment to
aging and illness is an important asset. Ailments are accepted realistically and local
physicians are patronized at will. Nonscientific medical beliefs have been observed
in Amish society, but what is most marked is an overall concern for the sick in the
community. Persons who are too ill to attend religious services are discussed at
great length by anxious friends. They are normally visited by relatives and friends
Sunday afternoon or during the week. Small gifts of food or other specialties are
often given to them. The senile and the mentally ill are cared for in the household
except when such care would be physically dangerous for the patient or his
caretakers. Special modifications may be made in the *Ordnung* for the physically
ill. The family and community provide the aged with a sense of belonging and a
feeling of being needed. Older people are more free to travel and consequently often
do more visiting than other adults.

Elderly Amish people are concerned with others beyond their immediate family, as well as with the welfare of the community and the world within their grasp. Interest in the well-being of others generally overshadows self-absorption and pre-occupation with personal needs and comforts. There is time for reflection and the enjoyment of many grandchildren as the individual's major efforts are nearing completion. In the final stage of life there is integrity rather than despair. The elderly Amish person looks back on his or her life with satisfaction and looks forward to life eternal.

Dying takes place in familiar surroundings rather than in a lonely, impersonal, and mechanical environment (Bryer 1979). Except for accidental or sudden illnesses, most Amish are allowed to die in peace and dignity surrounded by friends and relatives in their own house. When death occurs, few decisions need to be made by the family that are not dictated by custom. Neighbors and nonrelatives relieve the family of all work responsibility. Young men are appointed to take over the farm chores and an experienced couple takes over the responsibility of managing the household until after the funeral. These appointments are considered a great honor. The managing couple will solicit as many helpers as are needed for cleaning, food preparation, and making burial arrangements. The relatives spend their time in quiet meditation and in conversation around the bier where guests come to see their departed friend and to talk to the bereaved family. Some communities observe the wake by sitting around the deceased all or part of the night. Young people gather to sing hymns on at least one of the evenings before the funeral. In other communities several people sleep near the body. Amish coffins are made by an Amish carpenter or occasionally by an undertaker who caters to the customs of the local Amish community. Pallbearers are selected by the family. Their duty is to dig the grave, assist with the physical arrangements at the funeral, open and close the coffin for viewing, arrange for transportation, and close the grave at the cemetery.

Funerals, especially of elderly people, are attended by large numbers of friends and relatives from various states. As many as five hundred mourners may be present. Following the burial, it is the custom to return to the house of the deceased for a meal; at this meal normal role relationships and responsibilities are restored. The quietness and seriousness which have prevailed for three days is now broken by normal conversation and interaction. Family members are readily integrated into the ongoing concerns of the community where bereavement is healed by godly and ethnic ties. The belief in eternal life beyond death is also a source of comfort to the mourning family. Death shakes the emotional foundations of the individual, but the major burdens are borne by the church-community.

3 / The Rise of Amish Schools

The Amish schools were founded in response to massive consolidation of rural public schools in this country. The first Amish school was founded in Delaware in 1925. There were four schools in 1940 and by 1990 the number had grown to 726. In this chapter we will discuss the divergence which developed between Amish education and the public school system.

When the population in the United States was primarily rural and the major occupation was farming, the Amish people had no real objections to public schooling. Some contact in school with English or non-Amish children is still considered desirable by many Amish. In the rural public school the Amish child was treated as a member of a group rather than as a unique personality. The songs learned were largely religious; they were copied into notebooks and sung in unison, as is done in the Amish tradition. The Amish children achieved their basic skills in reading, writing, and arithmetic, and the school was acceptable to the Amish, even though a considerable portion of the program was neither meaningful nor relevant to the Amish way of life. The method of learning (orally and by example) was consistent with the Amish culture. So long as the schools were small and near their farm homes, the Amish were able to moderate exposure to alien values. With public school consolidation these conditions changed.

CONFRONTATIONS

Since the states rather than the federal government are responsible for the maintenance and operation of public schools, the laws which govern schools vary somewhat from one state to another. In most states Amish parents were arrested and charged with criminal neglect for not continuing to send their children to school until the required age. Basically the Amish parents objected, not to specific laws, but to having their children trained for a way of life contrary to their religion. A few examples of confrontations in different states between Amish and non-Amish views of education will illustrate the emerging differences.

In 1921 the Ohio General Assembly passed a law requiring all children in the state to attend certified schools until the age of eighteen and to study history, geography, and hygiene (Luthy 1986:513). A work permit was permitted at the age of sixteen. The Amish people refused to abide by the new law. They wanted their children to receive instruction in reading, writing, and arithmetic, but they told their children not to study other subjects.

Five Amish fathers were arrested for violating the state's educational law and were summoned to the Holmes County court. They were charged with neglect and refusal to permit their school children to study the subjects of history, geography, and hygiene. The children were taken into custody by the Children's Home of Holmes County, and the parents were ordered to pay for their stay. While staying at the children's home, the boys' hair was cut short, the girls' hair was braided in pigtails, and the children were dressed in "English" clothing, setting aside their Amish garb. It took two weeks for the parents to obtain the release of their children.

Thirty-five years later, in 1957, Amish families in Wayne County, Ohio were informed that children who had completed the eighth grade were not allowed to repeat the grade but must be promoted to ninth and tenth grade until their fifteenth birthday, necessitating high school attendance. If they repeated eighth grade, the children would be placed in state welfare homes. When six non-complying parents were brought into court they were supported by a courtroom filled with many non-Amish neighbors and local businessmen (Hershberger 1985).

The truant officer testified that six children were not in school. The judge reminded the defendants that he must enforce the law. Even though a child might not profit by going to school, the law left the judge with no alternative but to take action. He declared the six children "neglected" and assigned them to the county welfare board. Local merchants tried to approach the judge, but he left by the back door. The school board agreed to secure a vacant house nearby which would serve as a school for ninth graders where they would be taught English, home economics, agriculture, shop and science. The Amish refused. One of their spokesmen, Henry Hershberger said: "It's just a case of our religion conflicting with the law. We want to work something out so both can be brought together so we can keep the law without breaking our religion." Religion, he said, demanded that the children be in the home during their years of growing up.

On the next day officers of the court were sent to the homes of the defendants to bring the children to the county home. Only one boy, Emanuel, could be found. A girl, Delila, would not leave her home without the consent of her father, who was not at home. She was taken to the welfare home the next day. Some of the boys fled to an Amish settlement in Pennsylvania. The judge was incensed.

In the meantime, newspaper accounts began to report the "kidnapping" of Amish children, of the abduction of the children of peaceful people simply because they did not attend government schools. A prominent businessman and a member of the welfare board resigned in protest, charging that the county welfare officials were using the welfare home as a punitive institution; that they seized children from their parents, incarcerating them against their will and at taxpayers' expense. Education, the welfare officer explained, should not be turned into a device to inflict slavery.

Once again, the six fathers found themselves in court. This time the judge charged them with contempt. An Amishman asked the judge, "For what reason are you holding us in contempt?"

The judge answered: "You did not surrender the boy. When the court makes an order it has to be obeyed."

Mr. Hershberger then spoke up: "According to the church and the Bible I couldn't give my boy up and send him to someone else. Doesn't religion stand any more?"

The judge replied: "You must understand that your church rules will not stand in this action. The rules of your church cannot prevail against the statutes of the legislature." An Amish bishop explained: "We will give our children up if there has been some crime, but in a religious case like this we can't give our children away. It's a commission against the church." "All religions stand alike in my court," the judge replied. And to the surprise of the courtroom audience, he said: "My order is that they [the defendants] stand in prison until they purge themselves of this contempt charge."

The parents of twelve children were among those imprisoned. The oldest daughter, age 13, stayed out of school and cooked and cared for the children at home. The Amish spokesman replied: "We don't want to make a big thing out of this." A sympathetic Ohio attorney volunteered to help the imprisoned Amish without charge, promising to respect their wishes. The offer was accepted with qualifications by the Amish.

The attorney discovered that the Amish defendants had been jailed without proper commitment papers, that they came to court without benefit of counsel, and were not advised by the court of their right to counsel. The defendants, he said, were punished and jailed for indirect contempt by disobeying an order of court when no order had ever been issued to them. The Amish were released after having spent two weeks in the county prison.

Although these illustrations were drawn from Ohio, Amish in other states were experiencing similar problems. During a period of about thirty years, beginning in the thirties, at least twenty similar confrontations occurred in Lancaster County,

Amish parents, both men and women, were jailed in 1951 for refusing to send their children to public high school. (Lancaster New Era photo.)

Pennsylvania, as each township closed its small schools and opened a consolidated school. Amish parents were repeatedly sent to jail for refusing to let their children attend the large, consolidated school (Lapp 1991:191).

The Amish in Pennsylvania expressed their opposition to forced attendance at high school and consolidation. "We're not opposed to education," said one Amish spokesman, "we're just against education higher than our heads, I mean education that we don't need" (Kraybill 1989:120). Another said ". . . don't raise the school age for farm children . . . for if they don't do farm work while they're young they seldom care for it when they're older." The controversy came to a head in 1937 when school officials in Lancaster County planned to build a consolidated school and wipe out ten one-room schools in the heart of the Amish farm community. Fear that school consolidation would place their children on school busses and in classrooms with strange teachers, a group of Amish, on the advice of an attorney, obtained a court order to halt construction of the new school building. Some Amish had circulated a petition, gathering over 3,354 signatures which they pasted into a 130-foot scroll. Other Amish opposed such aggressive action, and in 1940 migrated to the state of Maryland where school problems were not an issue.

The Amish lost their appeal, and the new consolidated school was soon built. Amish leaders now favored a more gentle approach, but felt they had to "do something." They appealed to the Pennsylvania Assembly for leniency and exemption of their children from attending school after completion of the elementary grades. A group called "Delegation for Common Sense Schooling" wrote a new petition entitled "To Our Men of Authority" in hopes of influencing state legislators. The delegation to the Pennsylvania Assembly promised to defend themselves with "the word of God" instead of using the services of a lawyer. They also met with the governor.

Instead of gaining leniency, the Amish pleas were met with stiff opposition. The legislature raised the compulsory attendance age for rural youth to fifteen years and lengthened the school year term to nine months. This action convinced the Amish that they needed to open private schools for their children. They proceeded against the advice of state lawmakers. Arrests, jailings, and court action continued for another five years. One Amish father, arrested seven times, appealed his conviction as a test case and lost. Some parents had their children repeat the eighth grade to avoid going to high school. Others held their pupils back from first grade so that they would be fifteen on completing the elementary grades. Still others suffered arrests and brief imprisonment. Although the legislature passed a measure to permit the Attorney General to issue work permits for fourteen year olds, school authorities refused to issue them.

The Amish were not about to concede. They were willing to face arrest, fines, mockery, imprisonment and martyrdom if necessary. They appealed to the Bible, the teachings of Christ, the examples of the Apostles, the Anabaptist martyrs, their Amish forefathers, tradition, experience, conscience, and the religious liberty granted by the Constitution.

Finally in Pennsylvania a partial compromise was reached in 1955 with the election of a new governor. Governor George Leader said the problem was not with the law, but the interpretation of the law. His administration showed an attitude of conciliation. The Amish School Committee, the County Superintendent of Schools, and the Department of Education approved a vocational training program for children who had completed the eighth grade. Under the program, an Amish teacher held classes, three hours per week in an Amish home. The youth studied English, math, spelling, and subjects related to agriculture, and each of the pupils submitted daily journals of their work activities on the farm and home. Attendance records were submitted to the state. The solution pleased just about everyone. The state school officials could say the Amish were in school, and the Amish were able to control the place and the content of the education.

Early on a November morning in 1965, a school bus in Oelwein, Iowa, headed for the Old Order Amish settlement a few miles to the southwest. Aboard were a driver, a school nurse, a truant officer, and the superintendent of schools. Their mission was "to round up" some forty Amish children and bring them to Hazelton public school against the wishes of their parents and the leaders of the Amish church-community. Such decisive action was deemed necessary because the "plain people" had been violating the law by staffing their private one-room country schools with uncertified teachers. (Accounts appear in Erickson 1969:15–59 and Rodgers 1969.)

As the bus made the round of Amish homes, the delegation of public school officials encountered various forms of resistance. One farmer blocked his driveway to prevent the bus from entering. The superintendent entered the house and declared that, acting under the authority of Iowa's truancy stature, he had come to take the children to public school. The superintendent's efforts were of no avail. Parents reported that the children were "not here," and others had sent them to the Amish school. After the last home had been visited, the public school officials drove to the Amish school, where many of the pupils had already arrived. By the time classes were scheduled to begin, the sheriff and the county attorney were also on the scene along with a number of parents and children.

The truant officer entered the building and explained his mission to the pupils. Declaring that he was their friend, that he wished to help them, and that they would receive a warm welcome in the town school, he asked them to be good children and quietly file into the bus behind the sheriff. The sheriff started slowly toward the bus, and the boys and girls followed. Suddenly, either the teacher or one of the mothers shouted in German, "Run!" The pupils bolted for the rear of the schoolyard, scrambled through the barbed-wire fence, and ran through the adjoining cornfield into the woods beyond. Some did not stop running until they reached their homes. Only two children failed to escape. A 13-year-old boy who could not keep up with his peers was caught by the deputy sheriff who led the weeping youngster to the bus. A tiny girl of six never got beyond the cornfield, where she shivered and screamed. The superintendent took her to a heated automobile and tried to calm her. The delegation of school officials decided to return to Oelwein without the Amish children.

On the return to town that Friday morning, the truant officer suggested that "since the Hookies pulled a fast one on us, we should pull a fast one on them." (The Amish, who fasten their clothing with hooks-and-eyes because of their opposition to "ornaments," were called "Hooks" or "Hookies" by their Iowa neighbors.) That afternoon, when the parents were not about, the officials returned to the schools and succeeded in taking 28 children to the town school.

Iowa Amish pupils about to be bussed to a consolidated public school in 1965 ran into a cornfield. (Photo by Des Moines Register and Tribune.)

When the school officials returned on Monday to bus the children to town, they were met with resistance. In the meantime the Amish had secured the advice of an attorney. When the bus and its delegation arrived at the Amish school, they found the driveway blocked with a large horse-drawn wagon. The attorney for the Amish stood nearby and, reading from a legal document, made it known that anyone except the truant officer entering the private school grounds was liable for trespass. The truant officer retorted that he was allowed to bring assistants; the sheriff, who was also present, stated that he was responsible for upholding the law. He moved the wagon so that the bus could enter.

Guarding the school door were a group of stern-faced fathers. The sheriff and school officials pushed their way past the men—the Amish are pacifists—into the anteroom full of weeping mothers, who pulled at the sheriff's clothing and begged him to desist. He brushed them aside and stepped into the schoolroom proper. At that moment, the pupils began singing half-hysterically chorus after chorus of "Jesus Loves Me," led by a teacher who circled the room in distress. The superintendent attempted to pry a screaming schoolboy loose from a desk. Utter bedlam ensued as mothers rushed in to embrace their children protectively. Fathers entered to express their determination. The county attorney shouted his disgust at the way the Amish were behaving. So great was the turmoil that the authorities realized it would be impossible to effect a peaceful transfer of the children to public school. They retreated outdoors, and later that morning flew to the state capital for assistance from the state department of education. Behind them, they left an Old Order Amish community in a state of shock.

For a number of years in several other states the Old Order Amish were arrested, jailed, and sentenced for not complying with school codes that would adversely affect their church-community. Amishman LeRoy Garber, whose case the U.S. Supreme Court declined to hear, was harassed out of Kansas for not enrolling his daughter in a public high school. Another Kansas Amishman, Adin Yutzy, paid a large fine, sold his farm, and moved to Wisconsin to get away from "school trouble." When Wisconsin began prosecuting the Amish for not sending their ninth-grade children to public high school, the Yutzy family moved to Missouri. The school conflict has resulted in jailing for many parents. They have generally been released after friends and businessmen paid their fines. Sympathetic attorneys who have taken cases to court generally found no relief.

The laws in the various states pertaining to public control of private schools show a surprising lack of uniformity. In Kentucky, a jury found the Amish not guilty of violating the school attendance laws because "they acted on the basis of religious conscience." Maryland passed a bill stating that the Amish were a "bona fide church organization" and therefore not subject to license by the state. The Amish have had no school trouble in South Carolina, New York, Illinois, Missouri, Delaware, and Maryland. The Amish who moved to Missouri in recent years report that school officials are cooperative, and have sold good vacant schoolhouses to them that meet their needs. This stands in sharp contrast to the treatment the Amish received in Wayne County, Ohio, where a school board refused to sell the Amish an obsolete schoolhouse, even when there were no other buyers.

THE SUPREME COURT DECISION

In September of 1968, three Amish fathers from Green County, Wisconsin, refused to send their children to high school in the town of New Glarus. In doing so, they exposed themselves to criminal prosecution for defying the state's compulsory attendance law. The three fathers accepted legal assistance from the National Committee for Amish Religious Freedom, a citizens' support group that was organized the previous year when the Amish in Kansas and Iowa faced court action. The committee included scholars, religious leaders, and lawyers who were sympathetic to the highly publicized plight of the Amish people. They asked, "If it is lawful to be Amish, why is it illegal to teach people to be Amish?" Despite a series of court rulings against the Amish claim of religious liberty, the citizens' group secured an attorney to represent the Amish case.

William Ball, the attorney who took the case for the Amish, emphasized that it would have to be shown that there was a true religious liberty claim involved. Further, it would have to be shown that the Amish religion is an historically consistent religious tradition, that the Amish religion has binding requirements for its members, and that their belief is real and sincere. It would have to be shown that the state was violating the practice of Amish religion, and that the Amish, by keeping their children out of high school, did not present any significant threat to the state.

The Amish were brought to trial in March of 1969, in Green County, Wisconsin. Expert witnesses were called to the stand to explain the nature of Amish religion, to explain why the Amish children could not go to high school and yet could go to grade school. They were asked to explain the beliefs of the Amish religion, their education, the relationship between their belief and practice, and the educational choices faced by the Amish parents and their children.

Were the Amish people posing a significant threat to society by withdrawing their children from high school? The local sheriff was summoned to testify: "How many of the Amish youngsters of high-school age have committed crimes of looting, arson, rape, theft, drunken driving, etc.?" His answers were all in the negative. The director of welfare was asked: "How many Amish are in state homes for the aged? How many are in state homes for alcoholics? How many are on welfare?"

The state was claiming that the Amish children were being deprived of an education and therefore might pose a threat to the state. A specialist in private school education was asked: "Do the Amish receive an adequate education?" He testified that the Amish children were fortunate to be able "to learn by doing," since many high school students [today] lack a clear connection between learning and doing.

The county court acknowledged that Amish religious liberty had been violated but said there was a superior state interest in compelling the children to attend school. The decision was appealed to the District Court and the Amish cause was lost again. The appeal was taken to the Supreme Court of Wisconsin, which reversed the lower courts and held that the Amish children should be exempt. This court said: "Either the public school is irrelevant in their lives as members of the Old Order Amish community or these secondary school values will make all future life as Amish impossible to them."

To the astonishment of those who supported the Amish, the state of Wisconsin appealed to the United States Supreme Court for a review. The high court agreed to hear the case. Only a few years before, it had refused to hear a similar case in Kansas. The oral argument took place on December 8, 1971, and on May 15, 1972; the court unanimously voted to uphold the Amish claim (United States Supreme Court, *Wisconsin v. Yoder*, 1972).

The high court affirmed the responsibility of the state for the education of its citizens but said, ". . . the courts must move with great circumspection in performing the sensitive and delicate task of weighing a State's legitimate social concern when faced with religious claims for national requirements." Chief Justice Berger wrote: "There can be no assumption that today's majority is 'right' and the Amish and others like them are 'wrong'. A way of life that is odd or even erratic but interferes with no rights or interests of others is not to be condemned because it is different." The court said that it was highly speculative and without evidence to consider the possibility that some Amish children would choose to leave the Amish community and might be ill-equipped for life.

The state had argued that education prepares individuals to be self-reliant and self-sufficient participants in society. The court affirmed those propositions but held that in this case an additional one or two years of formal high school for the Amish children in place of their own informal education would not impair the physical or mental health of the children nor disable them to become self-supporting.

The court noted the successful and self-sufficient character of the Amish as an identifiable group during the course of several centuries. "The Amish in this case," the court said, "have convincingly demonstrated the sincerity of their religious beliefs, . . . the vital role which belief and daily conduct play in the continued survival of Old Order Amish communities and their religious organization, and the hazards presented by the State's enforcement of a statute generally valid as to others. Beyond this, they have carried the even more difficult burden of demonstrating the adequacy of their alternative mode of continuing informal vocational education in terms of precisely those overall interests that the State advances in support of its program of compulsory high school education."

The Amish people were profoundly grateful for the court's decision. Those families which had contemplated moving to Central America, Mexico, or Australia soon gave up their plans. One spokesman said: "We're not trying to get away from education. We believe in a good solid education. But in our own way."

SCHOOLS ON A HUMAN SCALE

Throughout this century the Amish have suffered repeatedly at the hands of school officials who had not understood their concern for education, or the distinction they make between technology and wisdom, between the critical analytical method and the quest for social coherence in their community life. The Amish schools today are neither parochial nor private in the sense in which these terms are currently used in America. The schools are built and operated by parents. They resemble more the pattern of the free schools or academies of colonial America than modern parochial schools.

The Amish community requires face-to-face contacts in order to remain viable. Its cohesiveness is based upon personal responsibility and shared values. The units of their culture remain small and on a human rather than an organizational scale. As long as the public school maintains this human scale, the Amish are satisfied with it. The Amish struggle to retain the school on a human rather than an organizational scale centered around several issues:

1. The Location of the School. The Amish insist that their children attend schools located in an agricultural environment close to their homes so that children can help with the farm work and aspire to become farmers, for farming is a basic tenet in the Amish way of life. Consolidation threatens the homogeneous character of the Amish community and exposes the children to alien values. To avoid these perils the Amish founded one- and two-room private schools.

2. The Training and Qualifications of the Teacher. To teach their way of life, the Amish want to have qualified teachers committed to Amish values. Their method of teaching is largely based on example and learning by doing. Persons qualified by state standards are incapable of teaching the Amish way of life by the example of their lives.

3. The Number of Years of Schooling. The Amish want their children educated in the basic skills of reading, writing, and arithmetic in elementary school. All training beyond that, they say, should be conducive to the Amish religion and way of life and under the direction of parents and co-religionists. Conflict developed over the number of years of schooling when states raised the age requirement from 14 to 16 and in some instances to 18 years.

4. The Content of Education. The Amish basically object to having their children trained for a way of life that is contrary to their religion. "Public or free schools," they say, "are intended only to impart worldly knowledge, to insure earthly success, and to make good citizens for the state." The Amish say it is the duty of the church-community to prepare their children to live spiritually in this life and for eternity.

Of six main arguments in favor of school consolidation (Loomis and Beegle 1950: 490–491), none were acceptable to the Amish:

1. "Equalization of costs between the poorer and wealthier districts." The Amish do not care if their district is financially poor, for simplicity and modesty are considered virtues.
2. "Better teachers." The Amish do not believe that higher education necessarily produces better teachers, nor that higher salaries insure greater competence.
3. "Superior curricula." The Amish consider the curriculum of the larger schools inferior, for it usually stresses science and lauds technology.
4. "Specialization of instruction and grading of pupils by age groups." The Amish are opposed to specialized instruction, preferring that their children learn only the basic skills of reading, writing, and arithmetic. They consider it a disadvantage to group children only with their age-mates rather than letting them associate in a mixed group, where the younger children can learn from the older and the older children can help the younger.
5. "Social advantages to pupils and to the community." This is considered a danger rather than an advantage, because the Amish wish their children to follow in their own footsteps and not to move on to other occupations or higher-status jobs.
6. "Better administration and superior vision." The Amish are suspicious of administration, for they believe that agreements should be informal and based on the word of the parties concerned. There is little need for administration in small face-to-face groups. The Amish also believe the vision of administrative officials to be inferior rather than superior, for it is usually progress-oriented and based on an exclusive belief in the scientific method.

The Amish were opposed to separating school from life. These were the alternatives: permit the children to attend the large schools (more liberalized groups have done so), request officials to keep the one-room school open, vote down the consolidation options and higher taxes, ignore compulsory attendance laws after the completion of eighth grade, or open private schools of their own. The Old Order Amish, who have no training in either secondary schools or college, responded to the challenge by building and staffing their own schools.

THE VULNERABILITY OF THE AMISH SCHOOL SYSTEM

The Amish school system is still somewhat precarious and open to attack by a variety of educational bureaucracies, and by regulatory and enforcement agencies. There are ongoing problems, and many of these are resolved informally by both the good will of insiders and outsiders. The Amish have little guarantee for the maintenance of their schools other than public sentiment.

The Supreme Court decision was a landmark case in the protection of religious liberty and parental rights. Not resolved, however, are other issues such as teacher certification and building regulations.

For example, in 1978 several Amish families, encouraged by the United States Supreme Court decision, moved to Nebraska to live, engage in agriculture, and raise children in the Amish way of life. They formed their own schools which lacked state approval. Criminal proceedings were brought against three Amish fathers on grounds that the school had no state-certified, college-trained teachers. The wife of one of the Amish settlers who had earlier taught in Amish schools was disallowed from teaching the sixteen children. The Amish fathers were summoned to court and issued heavy fines. Amish property was seized and sold at sheriff's sale. One of the Amish buggies brought $400, far below the cost of a new buggy. Mennonites and Baptists soon also faced criminal charges from the State of Nebraska. In 1982 all of the Amish families in Pawnee County, Nebraska, chose to leave the state. They moved to Ohio, Wisconsin, Minnesota and Missouri.

When the Amish first moved to Minnesota primarily from Ohio they found stiff state school regulations. Officials forbade the Amish to build or operate schools. When the public schools opened in the fall, the Amish appealed for help from their experienced leaders in Pennsylvania. The Pennsylvania Amish spokesman ascertained the approximate Amish enrollment, hired a chauffeur, and took with him two additional persons and a supply of school books used by the Amish. He then secured an appointment with the Governor's office.

The Amish met at the state capitol building in Minnesota with a group of school and government officials. The Amish spokesman showed the textbooks as well as blueprints of the Pennsylvania schools. He explained, ". . . our religion comes first, but we would not wish to give the state any trouble. Our people found many farms in Minnesota, and would like to farm them, but cannot, for religious reasons, meet the school code requirements."

After a lengthy explanation of Amish faith and practice during which there was "hardly a word said," the Amish spokesman concluded, "Since we cannot come up to the Minnesota school laws and since religion is the more important, much as we would like to farm in Minnesota, we will need to pull up stakes and go back to wherever we came from. We are indeed sorry."

The Governor's assistant jumped to his feet saying: "If you Amish wish to farm in Minnesota, and have one-room schools like where you came from, you can also have them here. If you will assist the Amish to do as well as they can, under their religion I will take care of the Department of Education." The Amish shook hands and left. Today there are twelve schools in Minnesota.

The Amish try hard not to confront and never to use the courts as a means of dispute settlement. They are morally bound "to live at peace with all men" and to "sue no one at law." But there are delicate issues which require negotiation, and a few Amish leaders have become skillful in managing these negotiations. The following cases illustrate extended bargaining sessions. The first involved a state regulation which forbade a stove in the one-room school. The second was a state-proposed plan to educate Amish teachers at a nearby college.

The Amish in one state were building a new one-room schoolhouse but failed to consult state officials for building permits or blueprints. When state officials learned of this violation they intervened. The state demanded that there should be no stove in the school room; that a heating system be either in a separate building or in the basement with a four-hour fire-resistant wall on all sides.

Amish religion and custom forbade heating a house from a furnace in the basement. They do not allow central heating systems in their homes and they do not want them in their schools. An Amish delegation met with the chief inspector and the Attorney General's office on four occasions. The talks reached a stalemate. The Attorney General sent a messenger to the Amish spokesman. The messenger was instructed to bring the Amish leader to the state Attorney General's office. He explained to the Amish that the Attorney General sent him with explicit instructions; the stove must be taken out of the schoolroom for "Where there is a stove there is fire."

The Amishman remarked, "Yes, where there is a stove there is likely a fire."

The messenger asked, "Will you accept this demand? What is your response to this request?"

The Amish spokesman explained, "I have no authority to accept this demand."

"Well," said the spokesman, "if you cannot accept, I must bring you to the state capitol for an afternoon meeting."

The Amishman replied, "I cannot come to the meeting today."

"But I have orders to take you," replied the messenger.

The Amish spokesman explained, "Since you require a 'must' there is no room to negotiate. So there is no point of my coming to a meeting."

The messenger replied, "If I get the Attorney General on the telephone will you explain just what you told me? There will be no telephone charges."

The Amishman agreed to talk. There was a long telephone conversation. The Attorney General explained, "Do you understand that we can close your schools if you put a stove in the school room? My messenger has school closing signs in his car. What will be your reaction to that?"

The Amishman replied, "The schools are a branch of the Amish church, and the schools belong to the church. If you can close our Amish church schools, that is up to you. However, if they will be closed, I would suggest that the teacher and children meet in the school yard or porch and enroll, and if there is a 'closed' sign on the door, we will not go inside, but dismiss for the day."

The official acknowledged, "This is very embarrassing. When can you come to the capitol to see us?"

The Amishman responded, "I would need first to meet with the bishops and some of the school directors."

The following week the bishops advised that since the Amish homes did not have heating systems in their house basements, they should not have them in the school basement.

When the Amish were later summoned to the state office they were asked about the decision of the bishops. The decision was explained: "The bishops have no authority to dictate. It is for the people to decide." The Amish explained that the bishops only suggest and the people make the decision.

After a few days the state proposed a plan. If the Amish would construct a basement and put a stove in the basement in one school (the one being built) the state would agree not to inspect future Amish schools. The Amish consented. Meanwhile, the Amish have not asked for approval of new school buildings and the state has informally agreed not to change the traditional Amish way of building schools.

A few years ago state authorities insisted that Amish teachers should obtain at least three years of high school before they are permitted to teach in Amish schools. Teachers and those who wish to prepare for teaching, they suggested, should go to a nearby state teachers college for a three- or four-week summer course after which diplomas would be issued.

The Amish leaders responded in a joint meeting with the Secretary of Education and the Attorney General that the plan would not be acceptable. The state authorities then suggested that the teachers come to the state office and take a three-day test to qualify as teachers. The Amish refused for two reasons: if those who took the test failed, then they could not teach, and the Amish did not want to obligate themselves to the state.

State education authorities then suggested that the Department of Education would supply teachers, persons who were experienced and certified. The Amish explained that they would not be able to pay the high salaries expected of non-Amish teachers, and that they were paying school tax and supporting their schools with parent donations. The state replied that they could find teachers that were sixty-five years old, and by living on pension, they would not expect high salaries.

The Amish said they preferred to have Amish teachers so that the pupils could learn to read and write German, and to sing and read their German hymns. The Department of Education, the Amish said, probably did not have the facilities to teach German script and to teach songs as they were sung in the Amish church.

Finally after several meetings the Amish agreed to try the plan, to have an elderly teacher come to the school and teach. The Department of Education sent a teacher to the Amish community. "She was a nice lady," according to one Amish spokesman, "and looked as if she could be a good school teacher." Amish school board members took her to a school where German and English were being taught. The session ended with seventh and eighth grade pupils going to the blackboard and writing their names in German script.

As the teacher was preparing to leave, she said, "I would really love to teach an Amish school but I could not do justice to your schools. I could in no way teach as your Amish teacher is doing."

The Amish spokesman replied, "When you return to the state capitol, tell that to those who sent you here."

Later in a meeting between Amish leaders and the Attorney General, the Amish asked, "Does a substitute teacher need to have a diploma or be certified?"

The Attorney General replied, "Oh no, a substitute teacher is taken when there is a shortage or when there is no one better qualified to fill the spot, usually on a temporary basis."

The Amish spokesman responded, "Our Amish teachers are the best teachers that we have or can find for a one-room Amish school. From now on our Amish teachers will be 'substitute teachers'."

The state authorities have dropped further discussion of teacher training.

The Amish in Pennsylvania, however, now issue a diploma, signed by three Amish school board members, to any Amish teacher who has had three years' experience either as a teacher or as a substitute. In Michigan, Amish church members have taught as teachers' aides and some Amish teachers in Indiana have taken the GED examinations.

4 / The Elementary School

ORGANIZATION

Amish society is localized, informal, and familistic. The administrative unit of their communities is the local church district; beyond the district there is no formal religious hierarchy. The various church districts and geographic communities are held together by kinship ties, visiting patterns, and by familiarity of belief and lifestyle. Just as the churches, which are self-governing units, differ slightly from one another on specific rules of discipline, so the schools vary in organization and administration. The schools have much in common, but since decisions are made locally, details vary from one school to another, from one community to another, and from one affiliation to another. The small size of the school makes management possible with a minimum of bureaucracy.

THE SCHOOL BOARD

All Amish elementary schools are administered by a school board. In most Amish communities each school has its own board, but sometimes several schools are administered by a single board. School boards usually consist of three members, with one of the members serving as president. Various other positions may be filled by board members or by other elected or appointed individuals. The clerk keeps records of the meetings. The superintendent, director, or committeeman attends meetings at a township, county, or state level; he is responsible for knowing any changes in civil law that concern Amish education and for implementing these changes in his school. The treasurer collects the money needed for the functioning of the school, pays the teacher's salary, and is responsible for paying all bills. Sometimes this position is divided into three: (1) an assessor, (2) a collector, and (3) a treasurer. The attendance officer is responsible for seeing that the children are not illegally absent from school and that attendance records are forwarded to state officials. In many schools the teacher forwards the reports, and the attendance officer is rarely called in. Some schools do not have an attendance officer. These different positions with overlapping rules and responsibilities may be confusing to the outsider, but the minor variations from school to school and from church to church are cherished by the Amish, who see in the fluidness of the organization a protection of their congregational social organization.

Winter snow storms rarely close Amish schools or interfere with attendance.
(Photo by Dick Brown.)

An Amish school district encompasses an area within a radius of "reasonable walking distance" of the school. Should the distance require transportation, the parents usually assume that responsibility. In some communities, the older school children will drive a "hack" to and from the school. The horse or pony will be housed in a small barn on the school grounds.

School boards operate informally with a minimum of rules and regulations. In each state the Amish have formulated minimum standards, and have issued "Guidelines" for the operation of their schools. Some of their standards are more rigorous than those in the public schools. For example, in Indiana the Amish require 97 percent of the pupils to be in attendance each school day. In each state the Amish appoint a representative to a national "steering committee" which meets periodically and discusses school issues as needed.

Board members are elected to their position by the patrons of the school, usually by a vote of all the church members of the district or districts in which the school is located. In some localities, however, the school is supported only by church members who are parents rather than by the whole church, in which case the parents elect the board members. When children of several different Old Order church affiliations (noncommuning churches) attend one school, the members of each different church affiliation may elect one board member. Old Order Mennonite pupils, for example, who attend an Amish school may have a representative on the school board. Women do not serve as school board directors.

Board members often serve for a long time. In central Ohio the school board term is decided by each district but is generally three years. In Indiana it is six years.

The man who has served the longest acts as president. He can usually expect to be off the board for one year between terms. Work as a school board member takes a great deal of time, energy, and personal skill, so a year of rest is generally appreciated. Church officials, who are often busy with church responsibilities, are rarely elected to school boards; however, in a few instances they do serve as teachers.

The school board hires and fires the teacher, pays the salary, enforces attendance laws, supplies the equipment needed by the school, and keeps the building and playground in good condition. It sets the tuition fee and levies or assesses the school tax. The school board meets as a unit with the teacher, ideally, once a month. These are open meetings and parents and other church members are encouraged to attend. The school board is responsible to the patrons, which usually also means the local church district, for the smooth functioning of the school.

Statewide Amish meetings are held annually for members of the school boards, committeemen, and other interested church members. Pennsylvania has held annual meetings since 1957, Ohio since about 1958, and Indiana since 1964. Within these three states, which have the largest Amish populations, there were statewide and regional meetings at earlier dates. The Amish church School Committee (of Pennsylvania) was established in 1937. Through the years it attempted to clarify the Amish position on education to state education officials.

In Ohio members of the church, both men and women, or members of the specific school districts vote for one representative from each township to form a State Delegative Committee to work with state and federal officials. These members are elected for a six-year term and are eligible for re-election. Continuity is

Parents transport the children in bad weather. (Photo by Richard Reinhold.)

extremely important on these state committees and most of the officers serve for a long time.

The state committees have several subcommittees. A small executive committee in Pennsylvania works directly with public education officials to make necessary adjustments between the state department of public education and the Amish schools. The officers of the Delegative Committee in Ohio have a similar function. These committeemen also meet with Amish in other areas who are contemplating establishing a school. A Pennsylvania subcommittee, the Old Order Book Society, is made up of both members and nonmembers of the state board. The original function of the society was to find and, if necessary, print books suitable for use in Amish schools. This committee also functions as a state treasury to help provide funds for the establishment of new community schools. Indiana has both a book and curriculum committee and a treasury committee. The treasury committee works on the funding of new schools. The curriculum committee works towards uniform curricula for the Amish schools in the state. The Ohio Amish have had a looser state organization. In 1960 their chief spokesman pointed out to the Amish School Study Committee of the Department of Education that Amish schools like Amish churches are self-governing units. Lack of centralization is important to both (Ohio Legislative Service Commission 1960:20). The Ohio Amish school standards drawn up by the state Delegative Committee have been used in Indiana and Wisconsin to help in getting state recognition for Amish schools.

In 1990 the Holmes County, Ohio, Amish community established an elected Delegative Committee and an elected advisory committee. The Delegative Committee works with state and federal officials. The three-man advisory committee represents geographically different regions of the community. Committee duties include helping teachers improve their skills and teaching methods, working with public school county superintendents, advising local Amish school boards about records and information requested by the county, and helping resolve any problems that arise concerning Amish schools. Two men who serve a six-year term are selected by the Delegative Committee. They are responsible for obtaining building permits for schools as required by state and local regulations.

FINANCES

Financial requirements are of two basically different types: (1) building or establishing a new school, and (2) maintaining an established school. Different methods are often used to obtain funds for these two categories of expenses.

The land is often donated for the school; money for the new school may have been raised by free-will donations, by taxing the Amish church members according to their property evaluation, by assessing each family head or each member a specified amount, or by a combination of these plans. Or the money may all be supplied by shareholders in the schools, in which case a part may have been borrowed (often interest-free) from church members. The building may be owned by the church district, by a few parents, or by a single individual. Generally the materials are purchased and the labor is supplied free of charge by the community.

Even with the large amount of donated labor, Amish schools today usually cost as much as $20,000 to build. There is a growing tendency for the schools to be financed by the whole church, rather than by a group of parents. In this way the financial base is enlarged. Thus, church districts group together to support their schools. At first these groupings included neighboring areas, then whole Amish communities; now there is an effort to have most of the cost of the new schools borne by all the Amish of a single affiliation within the whole state. Various settlements in Ohio each have their own methods for financing new schools rather than a statewide organization; money needed in excess of that provided by the cluster of church districts is supplied by the local Amish school board. As enthusiasm for Amish community schools gains momentum, there is a growing consensus that all Amish persons, whether or not they have children in Amish schools, should contribute to the support of these schools.

The operating expenses as well as the initial building expenses for the Amish schools are obtained in a variety of ways: free-will offerings by church members, assessment according to real estate evaluation combined with individual member assessment, and tuition. Often these methods are combined. If the school is owned by only some of the parents, then different tuition is charged to those who do not own a share. Tuition may run as high as $50 per month, but it is never used as the exclusive method of financing.

A teacher describes the tuition system in a community where it is used: "Each church member of both the north and south church districts pays annually for coal, repairs, and books. Any money left was put on the debt, and as that is now paid, the balance goes to help pay the teachers. Only those parents having children in school pay tuition, and it is the same for each family, no matter how many or how few scholars each has. Any orphan children's or needy family's tuition is paid out of the church treasury."

A parent describes an assessment system of support: "When money is needed, the treasurer sends word to the various church districts, and the fact is announced in church, and how much is needed. Usually it is so much per church member as often as may be needed. In the fall, and again around New Year, a collection is taken that is figured on the assessed property valuation." This system is the most widely used among the Amish, but the ease with which it is administered varies greatly from one district to another. Some encouragement is necessary for those members who are slow or reluctant in paying. In urging his co-religionists to help finance the schools, one Amish person pointed out, "You can't take your property to heaven with you—but you can take your children."

All the janitorial care and incidental labor on the building and grounds are performed cost-free. The physical plant is simple, with a low upkeep cost. The dedicated teachers serve willingly for relatively low wages.

Salaries for teachers are based on a per diem basis, but paid monthly. The salaries are roughly equivalent or a little less than what could be earned cleaning house. Male teachers, who are traditionally the bread-winners for the family, are paid more than women. Single girls who have taught for many years are frequently provided with living space or a small house of their own.

ENROLLMENT AND ATTENDANCE

The pupils in Amish schools are the children of Old Order Amish parents. However, "pupils from outside may be taken in by special arrangement if they are willing to come under the standards of the schools." The Amish are extremely reluctant to enroll pupils from non-Amish parents. A non-Amish farm family in Ohio asked a nearby Amish school to enroll their child in their school. The Amish school board reluctantly agreed. The state arrested the non-Amish parents for not having their child attend a state-approved school. The court upheld the right of the non-Amish parents to send their children to the school of their choice.

Although most Amish children attend Amish schools, there are many who still attend public schools. In exceptional cases several rural public schools have not been closed in order to accommodate Amish and Amish-related populations. In Geauga County, Ohio and nearby Amish communities there were 1,360 Amish pupils in Amish schools and 370 Amish pupils in public schools in 1990. Other regions where the Amish attend public schools in large numbers are Holmes County, Ohio and LaGrange County, Indiana. The parents reason that they cannot afford tuition costs. Others say they want their children to get "better learning." In some areas experiencing what has been called "suburban Amish," a high percentage of fathers are employed in the building trades and light industry and their children are more inclined to attend public schools than in large farming communities.

The Amish discourage home schooling which has become so widespread in America. They reason that learning to associate with other children should be part of a child's learning during the school-age years, and they ask: "How can children learn to associate with other children if they are kept at home?"

The Amish schools submit their enrollments to the state officials at the beginning of each school year and submit attendance reports routinely. They keep uniform report cards and a cumulative record for each pupil.

COMPULSORY AGE

The states determine compulsory school age. This has been the basis of much of the trouble between the Amish and the civil government. It was the major area of conflict in Pennsylvania and Ohio, a cause for concern in Indiana, Illinois, and Oklahoma, and resulted in litigation in Iowa, Nebraska, and Wisconsin. It is a point on which the Amish will not compromise; they will suffer fines or jail sentences and will migrate before they will capitulate. The Amish know that adolescence is a crucial age in the socialization of their children; they will not allow them to be socialized by the world during this formative period. They must shelter their children, not so much from ideas as from learning the roles and rules of the alien or English culture. The Amish consider high school to be a dangerous environment that is "a detriment to both farm and religious life." Not only do the children learn things they should not learn when they attend high school, they are also prevented from learning things they must know in order to live a successful life within the Amish community. The Amish respond to the problems posed by the compulsory age laws by having their own vocational schools, by obtaining work permits for their children, and in some areas they avoid high school attendance by not starting their children in school until they are seven years old.

AREAS OF COOPERATION WITH THE STATE

The laws in the various states pertaining to the control of nonpublic schools show a surprising lack of uniformity. In most New England states there is no regulation of private elementary and secondary education other than that the building must be declared safe by the state fire marshal and it must have adequate toilets, sanitary drainage, and a safe water supply. In contrast, many midwestern states have detailed regulations on compulsory attendance, certification of teachers, the curricula to be taught, and, in some instances, subjects not to be taught. Despite these regional variations, there are seven areas in which agreement must be reached between the state governments and the Amish: (1) health and safety standards, (2) length of the school year, (3) length of the school day, (4) attendance requirements for enrolled pupils, (5) age of compulsory attendance, (6) certification of teachers, and (7) curricular requirements.

The Amish cooperate cheerfully with these requirements except when they go against specific religious prohibitions. Certain Amish church districts, for example, forbid indoor plumbing. These schools have outhouses similar to those built by the state at roadside and state parks. Electricity is forbidden in Amish homes and is not installed in the schools.

THE PHYSICAL SETTING

Most Old Order Amish school buildings consist of one or two classrooms, often with an entrance room, sometimes a bookroom, and in the newer schools a finished basement where the children play during inclement weather. Rural one- and two-room schoolhouses were purchased from the state when they were available, moved if necessary, and often extensively remodeled. The Amish dislike the high ceilings typical of state buildings, so they often lower the ceiling to create a cozier, more homelike atmosphere. Today no old schoolhouses are available, and they build their own. The schools are well built of glazed tile, cinder block, brick facing, stucco, or aluminum siding. They are built to take full advantage of available natural light in lieu of electric lights.

Many Amish schoolhouses have old-fashioned, rope-pulled school bells. Doors open outward; the buildings are insulated and properly ventilated, and materials that can easily be kept clean are used throughout the schools. Schools in certain communities have indoor lavatories, but in most areas outhouses are preferred. The Amish building committees have their blueprints approved by the state officials and work closely with the health officers of the state "who know better than we do how a school should be designed" (Stoll 1965:61). The same set of blueprints may be used for more than one school. One-room schools usually range from 24 to 30 feet by 34 to 48 feet. If the terrain is suitable, the building is set true with the directions of the compass, for this helps the children learn directional orientation. In Kishacoquillas Valley in Pennsylvania all the schools are built with the teacher's desk and blackboards at the north end of the building because then "when the children face north to study maps, the lay of the county and the land will be imprinted in their minds exactly as it is." The Amish schoolhouses do not have the grace of early Shaker buildings, but they are simple, sensible, serviceable, and well built of good quality material.

The site of the school is carefully considered. Ideally, the school is located on a well-drained parcel of land that provides a large, safe play area for the children. If possible, it is located in such a way that all the pupils can walk to school. However, quite a few schools build small barns for the horses of children who come to school by buggy, and in Pennsylvania and Indiana some of the children ride to school on public school buses. Every school has a ballfield; some have as many as three baseball diamonds. Only a few schools have swings or seesaws, but activities such as sledding and ice-skating are considered when choosing a location. Parents graded the land at one school to build a sledding area for the children.

Typically an Amish school is entered through a cloakroom in which the children hang their hats, jackets, bonnets, and shawls, and store their boots and lunch buckets. The girls use one side of the room; the boys, the other. In some of the newer schools, wraps are hung in the basement. The main classroom is usually entered at the back of the room. The teacher's desk is at the front, as is a recitation bench. Along the front wall is a large chalkboard, above which is the alphabet and the children's names and grades on decorated posters. Along the side walls are large windows and either bulletin boards or chalkboards. In schools with cinder block or tile walls, all the walls are used as bulletin boards. The amount of decoration is determined by the personality and interests of the teacher and by the board that controls the school. The most conservative church districts allow almost no decoration. Only the children's names, ages, and grades, and such things as a calendar and spelling charts and perhaps a few mottoes are permitted. Compared to many Hutterite schools (Hostetler and Huntington 1980:67–74), where nothing is permitted to be hung on the walls or left on the top of the teacher's desk or table after a school day, even these classrooms appear to be decorated.

In most Amish schools colorful pictures and charts are on both the walls and windows, but the rooms are never cluttered. The impression is one of lightness, brightness, and order. Most often the desks and chairs have been bought from old public schools and refinished. They are smooth and shiny. The desks are fastened to strips of wood, four to a plank, so that the room can be rearranged, but the desks will not easily get out of line. Most teachers prefer these to individual desks for the children.

The large majority of Amish schools have only one room. Some are designed so that a second classroom can be added on. Two-room schoolhouses may be built with a movable partition that enables the rooms to be opened up for meetings and large gatherings. Occasionally, two teachers will teach in one large classroom, but this has obvious disadvantages. It seems to work most successfully when the teachers are husband and wife or two sisters who naturally team-teach.

CALENDAR AND SCHEDULE

The school year. The length of the school year is determined by the state. For example, Ohio requires 160 days; Indiana, 167; Pennsylvania, 180. Some states require that nonpublic schools have the same length of year as neighboring public schools. The Amish believe in a short year, with most of the hours spent in school during the winter, when farm chores are not pressing. They prefer to begin school late in August and to eliminate vacations so they can close in April. Most schools have only two days off for Christmas, one day off for Thanksgiving, and one for Good Friday. A few may close on Easter Monday or on "Old" Christmas (Christmas day according to the Julian calendar). Snow rarely closes an Amish school, for most of the pupils walk or come by horse and buggy or sleigh. Schools may be closed as required for major community events. Thus, the school may close when there is a funeral, because sometimes two-thirds of the children will be direct descendants of an old patriarch, and the rest will probably be related to him by marriage. More rarely the school may close for a wedding if the families of most of the schoolchildren are involved. If weather conditions cause cornhusking to fall behind schedule, the school may close for two or three days so the children can help with the harvest. These days are always made up, occasionally on Saturdays.

The reasons the Amish prefer a short school year are best described in their own words:

First: Although we appreciate having our own schools and teachers of our choice, we feel this still does not quite come up to having children together as a family unit under the influence of the parents. Having one more month of school would mean less family influence.

Second: Although we are a rural people in general, we realize there is a greater and greater need for a sound basic education. However, the old adage, "We learn to do by doing," still holds true. Learning from books becomes more meaningful as we tie it in with practical experience. During that last month of school our children would miss much of the basic principles of farming, that of preparing for and planting fields and gardens.

Third: We feel that our actual hours of classroom study in eight months would compare favorably with the average public school term of nine months. That is, counting such things as recreation during school sessions, basketball games, spring vacation, etc. . . .

Fourth: The nine-month school term is mainly intended for town and city children. We feel the extra month of school for us is not only unnecessary, but creates a burden and hardship to our way of life, in a spiritual as well as a material sense. We support our own schools, and at the same time support the public schools. This means higher taxes for us, and we are deprived of the help of our children at a time of year when we most need them.

Fifth: We feel that farming with tractors is not only impractical financially on most of our small farms, but with tractor farming we also tend to become more independent of each other, and lose much of the community spirit so essential for love and Christian fellowship in everyday life, as well as in the church.

Neither we or our school system is perfect, but it is our aim to raise and educate our children to be not only good Christian stewards, faithful to God and our church, but also to be useful citizens in our community. For this privilege we are willing to continue supporting the public schools through our taxes, and to assume the financial responsibility ourselves of educating our children (Eli Gingerich, *Blackboard Bulletin,* August, 1966).

The Amish school year is marked by special events associated with their studies. One is the spelling bee. The first "spelldown" (in Geauga County, Ohio) comes in February and the second in April. The German spelldown is held in the morning and the English in the afternoon. In April the achievement tests are given to pupils in grade eight. Most Amish schools have a simple Christmas program. Some have a spring trip of seventh and eighth graders and almost all have a picnic at the end of the term.

Achievement tests made by Amish teachers are given usually at the end of six-week marking periods and at the end of the term. Some teachers with the consent of their school boards give standardized tests (Iowa Tests of Basic Skills, Canadian Tests of Basic Skills) to their students.

At the termination of the school year, eighth-grade pupils are given a special examination. In one region in Ohio the test is given in two sections; the first section at the pupils' own school, the second section at a larger gathering—where the teachers take the test as well. At their own school the pupils write in alphabetical order the counties of Ohio and the names of the presidents of the United States in order of election; they draw a freehand map of their county, filling in each township, and they label an outline map of the United States with the states and capitals. Eighth graders from all the Amish schools in the county gather at the conclusion of the school year for the second section of the achievement test. This test is authored by the teachers, who submit 10 questions on each subject to one of the former teachers. Four or five former teachers get together and select twenty arithmetic problems, ten English questions, ten American geography questions, twenty spelling words, five questions each on Canadian and Latin American geography, and ten on Ohio history. The two-room schools in this settlement are built with a movable partition so they "can put it up for the eighth-grade tests." This community-wide effort of making and administering the test has proven to be popular among the teachers, pupils, and families.

Weekly schedule. All academic subjects are studied every day. Most schools have weekly spelling tests, usually on Friday. Friday afternoon is often special, with surprises and praise for work well done and perhaps a project such as making posters or changing the bulletin boards. If German is taught by a community member rather than the regular teacher, these lessons are held one or two afternoons a week, depending on the schedule of the German teacher. Those schools that have an art or craft period schedule such classes once a week in the late afternoon, often on Friday. In a few schools the vocational students join the regular scholars one-half day per week for classroom instruction.

Daily schedule. All Amish schools follow the same basic schedule, and it is virtually identical with that followed in the one-room rural schools of fifty years ago. The day is divided up into four major periods of approximately an hour-and-a-half each. Between each period is a recess or the noon break. During each period the various classes recite; generally about ten minutes is allowed for each class recitation. The children who are not reciting know when it will be their turn and what subject they should be studying. Questions from students in their seats are answered between classes, but rarely during recitation.

Most Amish schools start at 8:30 or 9:00 in the morning and finish between 3:30

and 4:30 in the afternoon. There is a 15-minute recess in the middle of the morning and the middle of the afternoon, and an hour break for lunch in the middle of the day.

Often the teacher schedules the subject she believes to be the hardest or the most important for the first hour. Some schools have reading first, some arithmetic. Spelling, generally considered an easy subject, is usually scheduled late in the afternoon, as are art or handicrafts, if the school has these, or various educational games or special projects.

All schools have an opening period that includes singing hymns, often in both English and German. The language in which these opening exercises are performed depends largely upon the community. Many schools recite prayers, usually the Lord's Prayer. In schools where the Bible is read during the opening exercises, students may read the selection from the Sunday church service in order to tie the school and church more closely together. Many schools have a song before dismissing for lunch, and some recite a noon prayer. Teachers may read to the children for a few minutes at the beginning of the afternoon session. Children often sing one or more songs before afternoon dismissal, and some sing as they file out of their seats to put on their wraps.

Although musical notation is not taught, singing is very important in Amish schools, and teachers are always interested in learning new songs and ways to encourage children to enjoy singing. Not only do children learn many hymns, but in some schools they also learn to lead songs according to the Amish tradition. The teacher sings the first note or two of each line and then the rest join in. All singing, except rounds, is in unison. Pupils who visit neighboring schools always sing together. The teachers, too, sing at their gatherings.

CURRICULUM

Amish elementary schools teach English (including reading, grammar, spelling, penmanship, and to a limited extent, composition) and arithmetic (adding, subtracting, multiplying, decimals, dividing, percentages, ratios, volumes and areas, conversion of weights and measures, and simple and compound interest). New math is not taught. Most schools teach some health, history, and geography; some teach a little science and art. Some very conservative Old Order Amish community schools substitute agriculture for history and geography. Reading is taught largely by the phonetic method; the children learn their letters and sounds before they begin reading. In grammar they learn the parts of speech and the rules of usage.

When the Amish schools were first established they used whatever textbooks were available. The families brought all the textbooks they owned, and from these enough were gathered for the school. In some areas local public school teachers and administrators gave generously in donating discarded books to the Amish school. Used books were also purchased at reduced prices. The older texts were preferred because they were familiar; they had been used by parents and other community members and they represented shared knowledge. The textbooks were selected on the advice of the former or present teachers. In Pennsylvania the Amish formed a committee called The Old Order Amish Book Society which issued a list of books for Amish schools. The Chairman of the Book Society obtained the copyrights to discarded public school textbooks and printed them in his print shop. The Gordonville Print Shop became the distribution center especially for arithmetic and spelling books and supplies. Among the list of favored texts were the *Scott-Foresman New Basic Readers*, and the *Strayer Upton Practical Arithmetic series*.

Reprinting the discarded textbooks from the public school was functional during the early years. The old books incorporated less science and fewer modern developments, such as television and computer languages into the stories. The pictures were also considered less offensive. The Amish are opposed to any sex education in school and to the type of health books that stress popularity and how to make oneself attractive. The Amish teach their children that they should adjust to others and not expect others to adjust to them, that one should not be concerned with how one can influence others, but rather how one can serve them.

Various schools use the *Alice and Jerry* series, the *Dick and Jane* series, and to a lesser extent the original *McGuffey Readers*. The teachers like to teach reading from these series, but the parents show some concern with their worldliness and play orientation. The stories in the *Golden Rule* series have a moral, but many of these are superficially patriotic or militaristic and are not appropriate for a nonresistant group that tries to live "separate from the world." The use of *McGuffey Readers* in Ohio during the early years of the Amish school movement is not surprising, because they were originally written by one of the founders of the common school system in Ohio at a time when the "notion that education itself was primarily moral, and only secondarily intellectual . . ." and "that the primary business of schools was to train character" was held throughout America (Commager 1962:viii). This idea of education coincides with the Amish attitude. Even the brand of patriotism expounded in the *McGuffey Readers* is shared by the Amish, for it is a "pride in the virtues and the beauties of the nation, not in its prowess or its superiority to other nations" (Commager 1962:xv).

Teachers did not like the *McGuffey Readers* as much as the parents did. They complained that though many of the stories were good, the vocabulary was difficult and outdated and much of the material was not very meaningful to the children. The first editor of the *Blackboard Bulletin* made a more basic criticism of these and other readers of the mid-nineteenth century. He noted that though the stories were highly moral in tone, the moralism was often worldly and materialistic. Of these stories he said, "First, they are not real to life. Good little boys just aren't rewarded with pocket knives and gold coins every time they overcome a temptation and do what is right. And I for one don't want my children brought up to expect a reward for doing good. Secondly, in most of the old stories the reward is a material one. This is wrong, it seems to me. The reward for virtue should never be a matter of dollars and cents. If there is a reward, it is a spiritual one first of all." (*Blackboard Bulletin*, May 1969:207).

The Amish have written and published two history books that are used in some elementary schools and in schools that teach ninth grade. They are: *Seeking a Better Country* (1963) by Noah Zook and *Our Better Country, The Story of America's*

Freedom (1963) by Uria R. Byler. Both include a fair amount of Amish history and help the children to understand their relation to secular history. One Amish author points out that the children should be taught that the early framers of the constitution worked long and carefully to protect the individual and the religious rights of future American citizens and that they began and ended each of their working sessions with a prayer. The children should know the full meaning of the efforts of these deeply concerned men, since they protect the Amish in their practice of religion and in their right to attend their own schools (Byler 1963).

The Old Order Book Society (in Pennsylvania) alerted school board members to watch out for a creeping tendency in texts produced by evangelical publishers. The frequent and free use of the words God, Jesus, or Saints indicated lack of serious respect, especially when the words "clown" or "monkey" appear in the same context. The emphasis on higher education and missionaries and their work was also found objectionable.

Most Amish do not want their children to read fairy tales or myths; many object to any stories that are not true, such as those in which animals talk and act like people or stories that involve magic, such as "The Pied Piper of Hamlin." The stories must not glorify physical force, nationalism, militarism, or modern technology. The subject matter should be American and rural if possible. Each story should teach a moral; those that are "just nice" are not good enough. It is difficult to find well-written stories that meet all these requirements. In order to meet this need, Pathway Publishers produced readers for Amish schools. The stories and poems, mostly of Amish authorship, teach moral values and Christian virtues of honesty, thrift, purity, and love—without undue religiosity. Some selections help children appreciate nature and a rural way of life.

The most dramatic change in the Amish school curriculum in the last two decades is the literary output of the Amish and Mennonites themselves. They are creating their own textbooks, teacher's guides, workbooks and tests. The more creative teachers realize that they cannot meet the needs of their pupils by using textbooks that are fifty years old, written for another time and another people.

Pathway Publishing Corporation was visualized during the harvest season by three members of the Old Order Amish Church and chartered in 1964 to "publish and distribute worthwhile reading material." Located in the countryside near Aylmer, Ontario, the corporation is operated by the Amish without the use of electricity, telephone, or any appliance using a digital display. To date Pathway has issued more than 100 titles. In addition to publishing early Anabaptist history books and three periodicals, they produced a set of thirteen texts accompanied by workbooks for grades 1–8. The *Blackboard Bulletin*, "a teachers' magazine which includes discussions, idea swaps, and true life stories of the classroom," has played a significant role in the development of both Old Order Amish and Old Order Mennonite schools and the education of Amish teachers.

Schoolaid, formed by five Old Order Mennonite teachers, has produced a series of books for teachers for teaching arithmetic, word study, English, geography, and a handbook for teachers called *Schoolteacher's Signposts,* and a *Language Arts Guide* for first grade. An English series *Climbing to Good English* is a pupils' consumable English text/workbook for grades 1–8.

Although they are produced by the Old Order Mennonites, these materials are also acceptable to the Amish teachers. The pointed introductions to these books stress the ideals which the curriculum must have. Teaching materials should have proper respect and reverence for sacred things. They should uphold solid "Christian ideals without actually mentioning scripture." They should teach right and wrong on the child's level, and avoid doctrinal instruction. The material should not conflict with the teaching of the churches. The teaching materials aim to give clear, complete, and simple explanations in concepts taught and in assignments given. High quality "seatwork" is expected of the pupils.

In their community schools the Amish children are presented with certain appropriate facts, which they are encouraged to learn thoroughly rather than to question critically. These basic facts form a part of their shared knowledge and thus help the community remain of one mind, so decisions can be made from a common core of knowledge. Amish pupils are taught correct answers. Even if there is a range of possible alternatives, children are generally taught that one of the possibilities "is right for you." This is consistent with the church congregation deciding as a unit what rules will be applicable and what behavior is correct in each church district.

What is omitted from the Amish school curriculum is as important as what is taught, for the school functions as one of the boundary-maintaining mechanisms for the culture, keeping the children sheltered from "the world." Most Old Order Amish attribute a positive teaching role to their schools, but a few conservative Old Order affiliations see the role of the school as primarily negative, its function being to remove unnecessary and dangerous facts from the children's environment. These churches do not want either geography or history to be taught, for both subjects present the outside world with its wars, intrigues, and technology.

Ideally the curriculum of the Amish elementary school helps the children to live their Christianity and thus eventually to achieve not historical or earthly acclaim, but eternal rewards. The children learn not to be overly concerned with their place in the world but to concentrate on preparation for eternity. They are told, "Do all the good you can, but do not feel important; this world would be here anyhow, even if you and I had never been born."

EXTRACURRICULAR LEARNING

Amish pupils learn many things at their school that are not strictly part of the curriculum, but that help them to become well-socialized members of the larger community. Amish visitors are always welcomed at the school. The children are quietly pleased to have visitors; the teacher greets them and introduces them to the children, explaining not only who the visitors are but where they come from. Usually the visitors say a few words to the children, and the children sing some songs for the guests. The children enjoy the interaction with the wider community and appreciate adults coming to their school. The children often learn something of other Amish communities, for the guests may be parents or neighbors or may be from out of state. Not only do adults come, but vocational students, recent graduates, and seventh- and eighth-grade pupils from other schools visit, adding to the network of relationships within the wider community. Schools exchange letters, and children have pen-pals in other communities whom they will one day meet. Some schools publish papers that they take home to their families and exchange with other schools. When someone in the neighborhood is ill, the children write letters and perhaps make a scrapbook or "sunshine box" for the shut-in. They will visit and sing for an elderly neighbor who is housebound. All these activities help the children to learn their responsibilities and understand their place in the wider Amish community.

The janitorial work is done by the teacher and the children. They tend the heating stove, bring in the wood or coal, pick up litter from the yard, and keep the schoolroom swept and the windows washed. It is their school. Their parents paid for it; they built it with their own hands, and the children and their teacher keep it warm, clean, and neat. This care and involvement helps to produce a strong tie of affection.

The children bring sandwiches to school, which they may heat on the stove and eat at their desks during the first ten or fifteen minutes of the noon hour. The rest of the hour they are free. When the weather is pleasant they play vigorously in the schoolyard, but during the winter there is a long time to spend inside. Schools with finished basements have lively games of various types, such as dodgeball or ping-pong games with as many as twenty children playing at once, circling the table, each with his own table tennis paddle.

They may play pussy-in-the-corner, hopscotch, red light, fruit basket, or blind-man's buff. They also play such board games as parchesi, checkers, Chinese checkers, Sorry, and carrom. Jacks and marbles are popular, and in some schools children play dominoes and educational lotto. They also put together puzzles and play chalk games at the blackboard. The youngest ones like to play school. Where available outside, play equipment such as swings, seesaws, and basketball hoops are popular; but nothing is as well-liked, especially by the older children, as softball. When there is snow, they sled and play fox and geese. Other popular games are prisoner's base, grey wolf, kick-the-can, Red Rover, Andy-over, follow-the-leader, and a variety of tag games. Children are encouraged to play as a group; they are not permitted to leave two or three children standing around, nor are they allowed to exclude one another from their talk or play. Some teachers use the winter noon hour to teach the girls to knit, crochet, or embroider. At times the teachers go outside with the children and often join in the games with them.

Teachers take their students on trips. They may take small walks into the woods to observe the fall colors and enjoy a picnic or they may go by haywagon to a neighboring farm to eat their lunch and watch the well-drillers. Sometimes the children in the upper grades go by horse and buggy with their teachers to visit other Amish schools, while the younger children are taught by a substitute. In some areas it is the custom at the end of the school year to take the seventh- and eighth-grade students on a trip. These trips last only one day, but it is not unusual for the day to begin at five o'clock in the morning, end after ten o'clock at night, and involve hundreds of miles of driving. One such year-end trip included stops at points of national historic interest, places of interest to the Amish, the airport, several small factories producing food products, an egg-grading plant, and the agricultural experiment station. Sometimes they go to the state capitol, or they may visit a hospital. They always stop at a city store and have about 45 minutes to look around and shop for souvenirs. The pupils learn a great deal on these trips, and they are long-remembered as very special days.

Such teacher-pupil activity in extracurricular learning is not only rewarding to individuals but the shared experiences help make the school an integral part of a culture that is supremely social.

LANGUAGE ROLES

In addition to the basic academic subjects, most but not all the Amish elementary schools teach German. Before the Amish had their own schools and still attended public schools, they often had supplementary German classes to help the children master High German so that they could read the German Bible. The Amish do not speak High German but Pennsylvania Dutch, which functions effectively to maintain the boundary between the Amish and the outside world (Frey 1981). The relationship between English (the language of the world), German (the language of the Bible), and Pennsylvania Dutch (the language of the home) is a subject of concern in many Amish communities. Pennsylvania Dutch is the preferred spoken language and is used exclusively within the household and community; it is the family's responsibility to give its children a firm foundation in the mother tongue. In addition, the children must learn to speak, read, and write English to live successfully on the margin of the twentieth century; it is the responsibility of the school to teach the children English. There is complete agreement among the Amish that only English should be spoken during all school hours except for actual German classes. But there is disagreement as to whether English or Pennsylvania Dutch should be spoken on the playground. The majority of schools encourage the use of English during recess, for the teachers believe it helps the children become fluent in English. However, some parents fear that the children are becoming too fluent in English and preferring it to Pennsylvania Dutch.

In order to understand the strong feelings aroused by discussions of whether or not to allow Pennsylvania Dutch to be spoken on the playground, and of how much time should be devoted to studying High German, it is necessary to know what English and German represent to most Amishmen. Joseph Stoll explains it well:

> As Old Order Amish, we associate German with church services and our home life—the religious and deeply moral part of our lives. German in a sense represents all that we have for centuries been trying to hold—our heritage as a nonconformed people, pilgrims in an alien land. It represents the old, the tried, and proven, the sacred way.
>
> The English language, by contrast, we associate with the business world, society, worldliness. English in a sense represents everything outside our church and community, the forces that have become dangerous because they make inroads into our churches and lure people from the faith. Therefore, the English language, though acknowledged all right in its place, becomes suspect when associated with the lure of the world (*Blackboard Bulletin*, May 1969:208).

Due to the close tie between the German language and religion in the minds of the Amish and to their history of learning German outside the schools, some communities still have members come into the school to teach German. Often one of the respected men in the community will teach German one half-day a week. However, as the total community emotionally accepts the school as an integral part, the regular classroom teacher is taking over the role of German teacher. In no school is High German taught as a means of oral communication. During German class, all oral discussion is in Pennsylvania Dutch. Though they do not know how to converse in High German, most graduates of Amish elementary schools are expected to be able to read the Bible aloud in High German and to love its cadence even though they may not fully understand the exact meaning of each word. High German is more than just another language to the Amish. It is the basis of their sermons and ceremonies, their religious oral tradition, and their collective memory and wisdom.

POST-ELEMENTARY SCHOOL

The Lancaster County (Pennsylvania) Amish maintain a vocational class for children who have completed the eight elementary grades but who have not reached their fifteenth birthday. As indicated earlier (Chapter 3), the vocational plan was a compromise between the Amish School Committee and the Pennsylvania Department of Public Instruction put into effect prior to the Supreme Court's decision (*Wisconsin v. Yoder*, 1972) that Amish pupils who have completed grade eight need not attend further formal schooling. Although some of the Amish communities in other states had adopted the Pennsylvania plan, they have since discontinued it. Pennsylvania Amish leaders feel obligated to maintain the vocational classes even though attendance is not enforced by the state.

Under the vocational plan, an Amish teacher holds classes three hours per week, typically for a dozen fourteen-year-olds in an Amish home or school. The plan specifies that a teacher shall teach "English, mathematics, health, and social studies, supplemented by home projects in agriculture and home-making." The students are required to perform farm and household duties under parental guidance, keep a journal of their daily activities, and meet in classes a minimum of three hours per week.

The vocational school teacher keeps a record of enrollment and attendance. Monthly reports are kept on record. Parents must supply written excuses for absences or tardiness. Report cards are sent to the parents monthly, rating the student on the following points: penmanship, reading, spelling, arithmetic, singing, German, homework, effort, behavior, whether the child pays attention, whether the child respects the teacher, whether the child annoys others or whispers, whether the diary is satisfactory, times absent, and times tardy.

The Amish are grateful for the vocational plan. Many of the adults who attended vocational school speak highly of their experience in the school. One girl said: "I am not sorry for all the German songs and verses I learned in vocational school. . . . As I go about my work I can sing many songs that I learned in school. It is a pastime to sing while you work, and it makes work seem like play just to have songs in your thoughts."

Through the vocational plan the Amish have been able to combine the teaching of technical skills and the job role. Techniques can be taught at the school, but competence in work can be acquired only by doing. There is a job etiquette that must be learned, and the best way to learn it is outside of the school, working at a real job in a protected and directed manner. This is managed admirably by having the children work under the direction and supervision of the parents. The young men learn not only how to perform a task, such as how to harrow, but also when to harrow, and how to integrate harrowing into all the other work associated with farming. The high-school-age Amish learn how to interact with other people in work relationships. While they are learning techniques, they are also learning a job role. Apprentice experience enables the young person to develop a realistic concept of what he or she will be doing as an adult. This type of schooling is related to life and comes close to the Amish definition of an educated person: "a man is educated who is on to his job."

These young people are learning not only how to do the necessary work but also when to do it, how to incorporate each task with other necessary activities, and how work functions both within their family and within the wider community. They learn to enjoy the work and to see it as creative, both in the immediate results and in its contribution to the comfort and happiness of others. This attitude toward manual work is a contrast to that taught, for example, in home economics courses in public high schools, where "in itself, it [work] contains no good" (Lee, 1963:183). In American high schools manual work is associated with efficiency but not with satisfaction. The Amish obtain greater emotional satisfaction from manual labor than do most public-school graduates.

After they complete formal schooling, individual Amish may take a variety of correspondence courses. In communities where a substantial number of young Amish people are employed in factories, a growing number are taking classes given by the public school to prepare for the GED (the General Educational Development test, which is also informally known as the high school equivalency examination). Taking this test is acceptable even though obtaining a high school diploma is not.

SPECIAL SCHOOLS

In recent years the community education of deaf, handicapped, and retarded children has become a subject of concern for Amish parents. In the past, deaf or retarded children were frequently enrolled in special schools which were part of the public school system. Some children were temporarily kept in boarding schools or were transported by train or bus to large cities where special help was available. They formed friendships with non-Amish persons and frequently left the Amish faith. Today all of the large settlements and many of the small settlements of Amish maintain special schools for slow learners and handicapped children. The enrollment ranges from three to twelve pupils.

The special schools in Pennsylvania are operated by a three-member Amish board. A ten-point guideline stipulates that they are not kindergarten classes, and that no child is enrolled without the consent of all board members. The age limit ranges from five to fifteen. The special schools in Pennsylvania are supported by the Old Order Book Society.

The largest special schools have three or four paid teachers. The children are transported by vans paid for by the parents. The teachers accompany their pupils during transportation. Deaf children are advised to learn sign language in regular or public schools before they attend the Amish school. Each child has a school desk except for those in wheelchairs. Teachers and pupils may sit around a low table to sing, perhaps using songs with motion as they sing together. The children are given paper and crayons and taught letters and numbers. All children are taught to write their name. They also learn by using flash cards.

One of the teachers explains: "Noon time is a busy time for the teachers. Ruthie has to be fed slowly. John can eat a little by himself. Most of the children need some help. After everyone has eaten and is cleaned up, the children are taken outside to swing if it's a nice day. At least two hours go by until they are ready to have school again. It takes about 30 minutes to get ready to go home. The children are encouraged to get their own wraps and put them on if they can."

The disabled, handicapped, and mentally retarded live in an atmosphere of consideration and affection. It has not been demonstrated that the Amish have a greater proportion of mentally retarded than other cultures. The Amish define a retarded person as "one who is not normal." This includes victims of birth defects, brain damage, blindness, polio victims, or those affected by genetic diseases. Retarded persons are not considered a social problem, for differences in ability and intellect are taken as gifts from God. Individual worth is not measured by academic performance or the amount of wages earned. The exceptionally brilliant child is occasionally viewed as "handicapped" by Amish parents. A "problem child" is one who is dissatisfied or disobedient and not one with a disability. The Amish do not believe that "hard learners" or even those "who cannot learn" should be excluded from group participation.

Special schools are, in the Amish view, very important. A parent commented: "It gives these children something to look forward to and enjoy. It is a place to feel at home and associate with others who understand. They have a better chance to gain confidence and learn to earn some of their own living. This makes a happier life which is a blessing for all. It gives the mothers a much needed break. Everyone has a chance to help along."

THE PROBLEM SCHOOL

What problems do the Amish have with their schools and what factors produce problems?

Amish schools are community schools, so any disintegration in the community is reflected in the school. Lack of unity within the community makes it more difficult for the teacher to have a school characterized by warmth and unity; cliques may develop among the children. The financial backing for the school is likely to be more precarious in a community that is not of one mind. In such a community the teacher usually does not enjoy the needed emotional and social support. Small settlements, geographically separated from larger ones, may have more trouble securing teachers; and the teachers, being somewhat isolated from other teachers, receive less help and support from their peers. Sometimes this leads not necessarily to poor schools, but to schools characterized by less variety of experience and less enthusiasm on the part of both the teacher and the pupils. Some of the smaller communities have less to offer the school in all areas of educational support. On the other hand, the new, small community may make up for its lack of members and relative isolation from other Amish with commitment and zeal. There is variation among communities in their attitude towards the physical plant of the school. A poorly maintained school, one that needs painting and perhaps landscaping, has more of an adverse effect on public opinion (non-Amish) than it does on the quality of the education the children receive. Schools that look quite dreary on the outside may be bright and lively inside. A few schools are run-down inside and out. A school board that is not highly motivated and unwilling to contribute time and energy is likely to have a poorer school to administer. A strong teacher and a few dedicated parents may successfully counteract a weak school board.

What are the weaknesses of the Amish school system as perceived by the Amish themselves? "Weak spots are beginning to show up in our schools after a quarter century," said one Amish leader in education. He said, "When our parochial schools first started, you must remember that it was a brand new experience for our teachers and school boards, and they just didn't know very much about running a school." Recognized needs are: "better teachers, teachers who have a good mastery of the English language, (no accents or slurring, no improper usage, no incorrect pronunciation of irregular English words), experienced teachers, and screening of teachers. Some people have the best of intentions, but ought to be doing something else."

One Amish leader observed: "Our school system is working, and it is working well."

Some schools are plagued with a high rate of teacher turnover. This invariably has an unfortunate effect on the children and makes it still more difficult to find a good teacher who can work with the children to build a good school. The quality of the teacher is crucial to the quality of the school, but even a good teacher can be undermined by lack of community support. There is considerable variation in the intelligence, skill, imagination, and dedication of different teachers. However, individuals who are clearly unsuited for teaching do not teach long in an Amish community. Very young teachers are more likely to have trouble than older teachers, especially in the area of discipline. One of the early symptoms of trouble is disrespect and poor discipline. There does not seem to be a difference between men and women teachers in relation to the quality of the school. A school that has become a problem due to poor teaching is relatively easily corrected; one that has become a problem school because of community disorganization is much more difficult to deal with.

Problem parents can undermine a good school. On a somewhat superficial level this type of parent does not help his children to get to school on time. A more serious problem arises if parents keep children at home when they should be in school. If a parent is uncooperative to the extent of keeping the child at home to work, then that child is transferred to the public school and comes under their legal jurisdiction. However, this is almost never necessary, for community pressure and reasonable persuasion is generally sufficient to keep, by public school standards, an excellent attendance record. Occasionally parents may undermine the teacher's authority and contribute to dissension in the school. A basically healthy community and a school with a good board can generally absorb a few such parents without undue harm to the school.

The Amish are competent judges of what constitutes a good or a poor school. They are aware of the factors that contribute to both and are constantly working for improvement. In an effort to determine whether it is possible for the Old Order Amish to provide an adequate formal education for their children, we selected schools for intensive study that were judged to be good by the Amish themselves. We were interested in the validity of their evaluation and we were interested as well in appraising the Amish ability to provide an adequate education for their children. We were not undertaking a survey of the schools nor attempting to construct a cross section. In 1971 the Amish school movement was so new that we were interested more in the direction towards which they were working than in making a total evaluation. We were impressed with how well these schools functioned and how few serious problems arose. We also observed, although we did not test, problem schools. We noted how problems were assessed by the Amish and how steps were taken that led to improvement. Because the school unit is small and the communities cohesive, problem schools can become good schools relatively quickly; and conversely, with the advent of a poor teacher, they can also deteriorate rapidly. As the Amish schools have become better established, and more completely integrated into the community, they have improved their ability to provide a good education for the children they serve.

TRAINING FOR COMMUNITY LIFE

The Amish school supports the Amish community and way of life. Although it embodies elements of the traditional private and "subscription" school, it is not a school governed by trained professionals, nor is it strictly a religious school supported by a centralized religious denomination. Amish schools are operated by parents who are members of the Amish faith, having as their intent the perpetuation of the Amish church-community. The school is an agency for the training and maintenance of a "redemptive" community. When the Internal Revenue Service sought to tax Amish teachers for unemployment and workman's compensation the Amish leaders explained that their teachers were self-employed and were agents of the church. They pointed out that their schools did not exist apart from the church.

The Amish school supports the religion taught in the family and in the community. "As the three strands of a rope depend on each other for strength, so the home, the school and the church should teach the same things, and not confuse the child, but strengthen its character and give confidence and security." Though the Amish school supports religion, it does not teach religious doctrine nor interpret religion. There is a strong feeling among the Amish that only the ordained, who have been called by God, should explain the Scriptures to an assembled group. Within the family the parents teach their own children but not other people's children. The points of difference between affiliations are so slight that it is difficult for anyone not directly involved to understand them, yet they can be of great concern to Amish individuals. Disagreement on small points of doctrine or application can lead to dissension. Intellectual discussion and argued interpretation of the Bible may, therefore, be dangerous to community solidarity. At informal gatherings people will talk about the Bible and refer to it, but in traditional Amish circles classes for Bible study are not acceptable, either within the community or within the school. The Bible used didactically, rather than ritualistically, is inflammatory.

The relation of the school to religious education is symbolized in a line-drawing showing education, religion, and morality conjoined, with the statement: "The constant aim of our schools is to fuse morality, religion, and education into one broad goal. The goal is to teach children to live that they may have eternal Life." Religion is central to the Amish way of life—the foundation of their morality and their secular education. Because "Christianity pervades all of life, it will come out in all subjects in school" and therefore does not have to be taught as a separate subject.

The Old Order Amish Christianity is primarily ritualistic and nontheological. Christianity for them must be lived, not talked. They are critical of the person who shows off his knowledge of scripture by frequently quoting passages. This is considered a form of pride, and pride in any form is despicable. Teachers are "advised not to include Sunday School lessons, nor induce the child to be Scripture-smart for religious show." In Amish schools Bible verses can be memorized and German can be learned from the New Testament, for like the singing of hymns, this is part of the ritual of the oral tradition of the Amish; it represents shared experience rather than intellectual analysis. In the same way, reading the Bible without comment, reading a Bible story during opening exercises, or the recitation of the Lord's prayer in unison are of this tradition.

All the Old Order Amish, even those who believe that the Bible should be studied in school, believe that Christianity is better taught by example than by lecture. "We can teach the Bible in our schools," said one Amishman, "but . . . if the Bible principles of love, forebearing, humility, and self-denial aren't practiced by parents and teachers, then I don't see where any Bible teaching in the school will have too much effect. A child will learn ten times as fast if the Christianity he is taught is also practiced than he will by merely being told how to practice it." Another typical attitude is expressed in a teacher's statement: "Reading from the Bible in school is necessary, but many feel that explaining the meaning should be left to someone else. We teachers could misinform the children." If the teacher is a woman, her status as a woman is a further reason for her not to expound the Scriptures.

The New or emergent Amish tend to intellectualize religion: "What Bible verse is applicable to the way I feel? Can I find the verse to tell me what I should do next?" In such groups the school also gives religion a great deal more verbal emphasis. But among the traditional Amish, religious expression is less self-conscious; because it gives an overall direction to life, small signposts are not needed at every crossroads. Their religion is not intellectualized, so it is difficult for them to describe their actions and beliefs logically, especially to those who are facile in quoting the Bible. This places the traditional Amish at a disadvantage when they must defend their position verbally. Realizing all too well this disadvantage, some Amishmen feel that they must be equipped to demonstrate their Christianity on all fronts and therefore that they must study the Bible intellectually, as well as learning it ritualistically. This feeling is more prevalent in the less-traditional community and consequently, the emergent Amish are more aware of their lack of training in intellectual argument.

PROVERBS AND WISE SAYINGS

Amish education is clearly wedded to what has been called "the living dialogue of the past" (Littell 1969:75) which has transcended the generations. Conclusions reached by the critical and analytical methods of science have small part in the Amish mentality. Like the Jewish oral and written tradition, the Amish maintain a strong group memory and group wisdom. The singing of hymns, retelling history, and wise sayings make up "the bread of the mind's life." As indicated elsewhere (Hostetler 1980:74) the Amish ways of thinking and perceiving conform to a "high" rather than a "low" context culture. Unlike personality types who are highly individualistic and somewhat alienated in ways that require little involvement with other people, the Amish are deeply involved with one another on many levels of communication. Not only do they make effective uses of their tradition, but they also incorporate present-day wise sayings into their value system. The examples below were gleaned from school mottoes, the *Blackboard Bulletin,* and Amish teachers' notebooks.

> Kindness always pays, but it pays best when it isn't done for pay.
> We are the master of our unspoken words, and slave to those that should have remained unspoken.
> A little sin will add to your troubles, subtract from your energy, and multiply your difficulties.
> To be contented with little is hard; to be contented with much is impossible.
> A smile is a curve that sets a lot of things straight.
> Life is a grindstone. Whether it grinds you down or polishes you up depends on what you are made of.
> Some people think happiness comes from getting. Others know it comes from giving.
> The branch that bears the heaviest fruit hangs the lowest.
> What we see depends a great deal on what we are looking for.
> Worry pulls tomorrow's clouds over today's sunshine.
> We show what we are by what we do with what we have.
> To know how sweet your home may be, just go away, but keep the key.
> When we are right we can afford to keep our temper. When we are wrong we can't afford to lose it.
> A mule cannot kick while he's pulling. Nor can he pull while he's kicking.

It takes less time to do something right than to explain why you did it wrong.
Walking fast doesn't help as much as starting on time.
Worry is just like a rocking horse. It keeps you going, but it gets you nowhere.
Being ignorant is not so much a shame as being unwilling to learn.
Happiness is found along the way; not at the end of the road.
If we would speak as kindly of the living as we do of the dead, there would be less gossiping among us.
Our conscience is the watchdog that barks at sin.
No people get less praise than those who ask for it.
Some people, like flowers, give pleasure just by being there.
It may be nice to be important but it is more important to be nice.
There is a wrong way to do right, but never a right way to do wrong.
It is difficult to learn what we think we already know.
The greatest treason is doing a good deed for the wrong reason.
Intelligence is like a river. The deeper it flows, the less noise it makes.
If you don't understand my silence, you won't understand my words either.
A good rule for going through life is to keep the heart a little softer than the head.
Mistakes aren't all bad. Remember that Columbus discovered America by mistake.
People don't care how much you know until they know how much you care.
Happiness is like a flower. It grows where it is planted.
No one is more confusing than the man who gives good advice but sets a poor example.
Contentment consisteth not in great wealth, but in few wants.
Good fences make good neighbors.
A lie stands on one leg, the truth on two.
A face without a smile is like a lantern without a light.
It is good to help a friend, but nobler to conceal it.
There are hundreds of languages in the world, but a smile speaks all of them.
I am only me, but I'm still someone.
The foundation of understanding is the willingness to listen.
Some minds are like concrete, thoroughly mixed and permanently set.

Tobacco is a filthy weed.
From the devil comes its seed.
It stains your fingers and your clothes,
And makes a smokestack of your nose.

5 / The Amish Teacher

ROLE EXPECTATIONS

Qualification for teaching in Amish society does not require the acquisition of a college degree. Suitability for teaching in Amish society is best understood by contrasting the role expectations of an Amish elementary school teacher with that of the typical American suburban elementary school teacher.

Just as there are enormous variations in cultures, there are preferred ways in which people educate their children. Amish culture is characteristic of a "high" rather than a "low" context culture (Hall 1976:74–77). In a high context culture individuals are deeply involved with one another. Awareness of situations, experience, activity and one's social standing are quickly recognized. There are many levels of communication—overt and covert, implicit and explicit signs, symbols and body gestures, and agreement about what one may or may not talk about. Members are sensitive to a screening process that distinguishes the behavior of insiders from outsiders. Unstated and nonverbal conveyors of information are extremely important. High context cultures are integrated and members think in ways that support the common good.

All of this contrasts with low context culture which, as in modern industrialized America, values literacy, rationality, logic, and individuality. People live more fragmented rather than integrated lives. Written rather than spoken forms of communication become very important. Persons are prone to learn patterns of manipulation to achieve their personal goals. Failures and alienation are blamed on "the system," and in time of crisis individuals expect help from institutions rather than from persons.

The role expectations of the Amish teacher are determined by the key values of Amish culture and by the stated or unstated goals of education in Amish culture. We pointed out in Chapter 1 that the goals of Amish education stress "humility, simplicity, and respect for the Creator." Members of the Amish faith speak about "our Amish way of life" in contrast to "the way of the world."

The qualifications of an Amish teacher as stated in *Guidelines* (1978:12) includes: "Good Christian character, good educational background, and a desire to improve that education." Other qualities mentioned are the ability to "get along" with children, willingness to cooperate with parents and school board members, a sincere attachment to the teaching profession, "and above all [the realization] that she will need help from a higher power to mold the lives of these children as we desire them to be."

Old Order Mennonite teacher instructs Amish children.
(Lancaster New Era, photo by Martin Heisey.)

The Amish teacher is expected to teach with his or her whole life. The teacher should be a person integrated with himself and with the ways of the community, for every aspect of the teacher's behavior and personality is related to teaching. He or she must be well-grounded in his religious faith and completely committed to the Amish way of life, accepting the limits set by the *Ordnung* and exemplifying the Amish traits of humility, obedience, steadfastness, and love for fellow man. In addition, a teacher must be interested in education and have sufficient factual knowledge to provide a substantial margin of knowledge between him or herself and the students. In other words, the teacher must be an example, and must be capable and of sound character.

The Amish attitude toward qualification and certification is expressed by an experienced teacher: "It is essential that we have qualified teachers. By that I do not mean certified ones, for state-certified teachers do not qualify for teaching in our schools." The Amish, who have effectively kept electronic images outside of their daily life, have been minimally affected by the communications revolution. They have limited the printed word, screening out much of the material that flows from the world's printing presses. They have excluded television. In maintaining a primitive type of Christian church, they have kept an oral tradition and an orientation to life that is relational rather than analytical (Cohen 1969). By its very nature, oral tradition is social; it is tied to the community. The oral tradition requires personal interaction, and teaching within this tradition is by example as well as by word.

The role expectations of the teacher in a low context culture such as in the American public school system stand in sharp contrast to Amish expectations. By the time bright children in public school have reached fifth grade they may know more about certain details and even areas of knowledge than a teacher. The prevalence of television, ease of travel, and the availability of books stimulate children's curiosity and enable many of them to pursue their interests to a remarkable degree. The public school system emphasizes the development of the pupil's rational powers. The amount of factual material that children are taught steadily increases as the total amount of knowledge increases and as society becomes more complex. For these reasons, it is essential that public school teachers be trained in many specialized topics.

Outside the classroom, the public school teacher disappears from the life of the pupils. The pupils rarely know what the teacher believes about religion or politics or where the teacher lives. The teacher's beliefs may, in fact, have little influence on the subject matter taught. The public school teacher must be competent in the subject matter and able in his teaching methods, for at least superficially, the teacher is hired to teach technology rather than wisdom. Most public schools do not want the teacher to teach attitudes or beliefs, other than the belief in scientific method and in our form of government. They want the teacher to stick to the subject: teach the children the material, but not how, in a moral sense, the material should be used. The teacher is an authority on subject matter; his authority comes from his training, and most of that comes from books. The printed word—and specifically the most recently printed word—is the final authority in most American classrooms.

All eight grades share one classroom and one teacher. Order, personal responsibility, consideration for others, and cooperation contribute to the smooth functioning of the multigrade school room. (Lancaster New Era, photo by Martin Heisey.)

The approach of certified teachers in public schools is mainly cerebral (understanding oriented) while in Amish culture the approach to subject matter is visceral (identification oriented). Both qualities are essential to cultural integrity and continuity. Teachers who understand but who do not identify with the community are at a serious disadvantage when they confront children and parents who differ from them in race, class, culture, or ethnicity. Trained middle-class teachers are too far removed from the oral or "wisdom" tradition to identify with the Amish and in most instances they are unsuitable as examples.

Because the Amish teacher's role is primarily that of Christian example rather than authority in subject matter they are not likely to present themselves to the children as "gods, all-knowing, all-powerful, always rational, always just, always right" (Holt 1964:171). They freely admit their human weaknesses and the need to turn to the "Master Teacher" for help and guidance.

TEACHER SELECTION

The Amish regard teaching with such importance that it is considered a calling rather than a job. Their ministers are called; that is, they do not themselves choose to be ministers, but are chosen by the congregation of God through the working of the lot. Similarly, an Amish person usually does not apply for his first teaching job; rather, he is approached by the school board. One girl said they had "been after" her for about six years before she decided she was ready to teach. When she did decide, she spent several weeks with various good teachers in the area, observing and helping for a week in each school. If the prospective teacher is younger than twenty-one, the father is asked, rather than the girl or boy directly, since an Amish person is under the care of parents socially and financially until then. One young teacher who had enjoyed her year of teaching said she was trying to persuade her father to let her teach the next year, but she could "bring so much more money home if I clean house and baby-sit and we don't have much money, so that maybe I'll have to do housework instead." In such a case the school board may try to remind the father how important it is to have good teachers in the Amish school. Teachers who have taught successfully are believed to have demonstrated that they have a calling, and if they wish to change jobs, they can apply to another school. However, the teachers' grapevine is sufficiently effective that the information is usually passed around informally, enabling the school board to make the initial move. A good teacher may receive as many as six or seven requests, even if the teacher has not indicated an interest in changing schools. These requests are written in such a way that they are very difficult to turn down. The relationship between teacher and school board, both by letter and when the school board calls, is a very personal one and does not in any way resemble a business agreement.

Amish teachers are not motivated by monetary rewards. They do not have contracts, nor do they have tenure. Life is uncertain, and no one knows when it will change. Perhaps the teacher will be needed somewhere else. If a parent falls sick, for instance, a teacher may have to stop teaching to care for him or her; or a young man who has been teaching may have to stop to take over his father's farm. The same principle applies if the teacher turns out to be unsuccessful. He or she is asked to leave. This is considered unfortunate, for it is hard on the children. If a teacher, however, cannot handle the work, it is obvious God did not intend for that person to teach and that it would be better for everyone for such a person to do something else. Amish persons who remain teachers do so because they have demonstrated talent and because generally they want to teach.

TEACHER TRAINING

The Amish have developed several semi-institutionalized means of training. Every teacher has had eight years of formal elementary education. Today most are the products of the Amish school system. Persons in Pennsylvania who have either assisted teachers or have taught for three years are issued a teacher's diploma signed by the Amish School Committee. The *Guidelines* (1978) state that teachers should use the vacation months to study the graded subjects, and should engage in self-directed research in order to maintain a "margin of knowledge." Many teachers take correspondence courses.

The first national annual meeting of teachers was begun in 1954. Not only teachers, but school board members, ordained ministers, beginning teachers, and retired teachers come to the meeting. From four-to eight-hundred persons attend. A small printed program is distributed to all registrants, giving the speakers' names, and often the names of persons who will lead small discussion groups, or serve on a panel that will entertain questions from the audience. The meeting is usually held in the summer, often in a barn or shed that accommodates seating for all. Meals and lodging are arranged by the host community. Hot food is prepared in the farmhouse and served on trays to persons waiting in line. Many gather under shade trees or sit on benches to eat their meal and talk informally. The atmosphere of the gathering has the seriousness, motivation, and enchantment of a barn-raising.

Since national meetings have become too large and the distances are great, regional meetings have been organized. Each state or area has formed separate teachers' gatherings. These large gatherings help to unify and solidify the Amish school movement, since both the ordained leadership as well as the teachers and board members attend meetings. There are also small gatherings of teachers in local regions. Teachers support one another by circle letters, visits to one another's schools, and frequent informal gatherings. A teacher who attended the first meeting and almost every one since wrote, "I believe these meetings have done more to create a better understanding of school matters than anything else." The two days are very full, but are pleasant and rewarding. Teachers from all states where the Amish live have an opportunity to meet one another and to talk informally as well as to listen to formal presentations on topics of practical interest.

Teachers' meetings function to bring teachers together to discuss their problems and successes. They help the teachers realize that others have similar trials and practical solutions. They function as training seminars in which the teachers learn how to handle their role. The teachers leave these meetings encouraged and anticipating ways they can improve their teaching and their schools.

Beginning teachers are aided by those with years of experience. They give this advice:

Pitfalls To Avoid

1. *Don't be bashful.*
A teacher must have backbone and not be afraid to speak with firmness and authority when children overstep the rules. Your pupils will try you out, if not the first day then certainly within the first week, to see if you mean what you say. Remember that every inch of ground lost must be recovered.

2. *Don't be bossy.*
The voice of authority is not loud, overbearing, or sarcastic. It is firm and loving, and shows regret. Sometimes words are not even necessary. A good rule to follow is, "Don't waste words when a look will suffice."

3. *Don't be openly suspicious.*
Learn to be a secret detective. Watch things out of the corner of your eye. Listen to what your children say, and what they don't say. A good teacher has her eyes and ears open, but she will not bark until she is sure she has something to bark at. Few things ruin teacher-pupil relationships like false accusations.

4. *Don't be afraid to admit a mistake.*
If you have accused a child who is not guilty, apologize. If you have made a mistake in any other way, apologize. If the mistake is a funny one, laugh and allow the children to laugh *with* you. If you don't they will soon be laughing *at* you behind your back.

5. *Don't be afraid to say, "I don't know."*
Teachers are supposed to know everything, but they don't. Don't be afraid to say, "I don't know." But don't stop there. Say, "Let's find out," and then help your pupil find the answer, in the dictionary, in the encyclopedia, or wherever the answer is to be found.

6. *Don't be too chummy with your pupils.*
Be your pupils' friend, but not their chum. You must not lower yourself to their level in the sense that you cannot step up and use your authority when necessary. This might be in sharing personal thoughts and feelings, in matching your physical strength with theirs, or even in various types of contests. Remember, you are the teacher; they are the pupils. The challenge is to use and not misuse your authority over them.

7. *Never belittle a pupil in the presence of his peers.*
This can be through scolding, ridiculing his behavior, or shaming him about sloppy work. Usually talking privately with erring pupils brings better results, and closer ties between the teacher and pupil.

8. *Don't expect to become a teacher overnight.*
You will have to grow into your work. Be patient when things do not go well at first. Seek guidance from God, advice from a fellow teacher, and keep on trying. You will hardly ever become the teacher you long to be, but things will gradually go more smoothly for you, until one day you will realize that you are enjoying your work more and more.

May God bless your efforts and help you have a successful term, and many more to come!

The Amish teachers' journal, *Blackboard Bulletin,* is an important publication serving the Amish school movement. It has a circulation of about 15,900. In keeping with the Amish tradition, its format is simple. Each year a list of schools is published. As the Amish schools become more institutionalized and the number of teachers increases, a limited professionalism has developed.

Not only does the teachers' monthly journal address practical questions—how to handle a mischievous pupil, whether to pass a seventh grader who does poorly in all subjects—but every issue also gives strong moral encouragement.

The contributors to the school journal are teachers, parents, and concerned Amish people, many of whom are widely read and value a good academic foundation. The editors have been careful to represent various Amish attitudes and have not been dogmatic in either their writings or their selections. The more conservative viewpoint is probably underrepresented from the perspective of the total Old Order Amish culture. The most conservative individuals are not as motivated to write and are not as committed to an excellent school program. They still regard the school as a peripheral rather than an integral part of the community. Sensitive leadership and selfless hard work have produced a journal and a movement within the Amish culture that is meaningful to Amish people of the twentieth century.

Teacher training among the Amish continues to be primarily informal and self-directed. Some of the teachers work as helpers for a year or two before they take charge of a school. The apprentice system works well for the younger teachers, who serve full time under the direction of an experienced teacher. A helping teacher often takes charge of the school for several days. The apprentice has the opportunity to learn how to manage a school while the senior teacher is available. Some of the teachers continue to take correspondence courses, although actual completion of high school is discouraged. The Amish feel that certain of the required courses are of no benefit to them and that to work for a diploma is therefore a form of pride. The best preparation for teaching from the Amish point of view, in addition to the personal attributes of patience and a love of children and learning, is a firm grounding in the Amish faith. Informal means are used to train future teachers and to develop interest in teaching. Experienced teachers may talk to individual students whom they think would make good teachers.

The informal support among Amish teachers constitutes a form of on-the-job teacher training. When they live near enough to one another, they may gather informally for supper every week or two and spend the evening with one another discussing school problems. The newer teachers visit the older teachers to ask about teaching methods and to learn such things as how to prepare a six-weeks test. Teachers compare parents and board members, problems and pleasures. They never meet without discussing aspects of school. Teachers may make friendship quilts for one another. Each teacher makes a square for the quilt. The teacher whose quilt it is sets it up in a frame and all the contributors gather for a quilting to finish the gift. Many teachers belong to one or more circle letters in which they discuss episodes and problems too personal or specific to be published in the *Blackboard Bulletin.*

Some professionalism is unavoidable, and in fact is desirable, even within this small, homogeneous subculture. As one Amish teacher put it, "It seems that after teaching school a while, a person gets a little hard to understand sometimes. And no wonder. Teaching is so far removed from farming or housekeeping that it takes just a little different kind of thinking, which is reflected in everyday living." Amish schools have a minimal bureaucracy that has no chance of growing into unworkable proportions. When the usual question is asked, "How can we improve our schools?" the answers are not those of an administrator or technician who thinks in terms of curriculum, buildings, or equipment. The Amish think in terms of character improvement, experience, knowing the pupils better, and bettering relations between teacher, pupils, parents, and board members.

SCHOOL MANAGEMENT AND TEACHING METHODS

An Amish teacher's way of life and his teaching methods are in agreement. The teacher teaches primarily by being an exemplary individual in close contact with the children. The teacher is a role model. But he or she is more than a role model, for a teacher imparts facts as well as attitudes and beliefs about how these facts should be used and how they fit into an Amish world view. A teacher creates the atmosphere of the school. The teacher is the shepherd, the responsible adult who is older and more experienced and knows better than the children what is good for them. The classroom runs smoothly because the teacher does not pretend that the children make the decisions. An Amish teacher quietly tells a child what to do and the child does it. Obedience and order are basic to a good school not just part of the time but all of the time. A biblical phrase, "Let everything be done decently and in order" (I Cor. 14:40), is a motto on the wall of some classrooms; "For God is not the author of confusion, but of peace" (I Cor. 14:33) is recited by the pupils. Orderliness is believed to make for more security and less tension in the pupils' lives.

Amish teachers instruct their children to "Do unto others, as you would have others do unto you." This quotation "should be placed in front of the schoolroom where all children can see and study it, and the teacher should quite often point to it as a reminder that this Golden Rule should be followed at all times" (Byler 1969). The Golden Rule is not compatible with individualistic competition. The Amish teach a nonexploitive value system by emphasizing individual responsibility rather than self-assertiveness. The Amish schools avoid the contradiction that Jules Henry (1963:295–297) speaks of where, in many modern public schools, the children are simultaneously taught to compete and to have love for one another. There is some competition in the Amish schools, but it is usually structured to support the group. The children will try to have better attendance this week than last week, better spelling scores this month than last month. They may even vie with another school for good attendance, or the teacher may post weekly spelling scores from a school where she taught some years before and the children, as a school or as a class, will try to do better than her former pupils. The children encourage one another's good performance so that their whole class or their school may do well.

The Amish believe that an individual's talents are God-given; therefore, no one should be praised if he is an easy learner nor condemned if he is a slow learner. These differences in talent are God's will, and there is a place for each person God created. The teachers and children are tolerant of such differences. All children are expected to work hard and use their time well; they are not all expected to master the same amount of material. Their differences are not concealed, for though slowness in intellectual learning makes for added difficulties, it is nothing to be ashamed of. A motto displayed in one Amish school says,

Little children you should seek
Rather to be good than wise;
For the thoughts you do not speak
Shine out in your cheeks and eyes.

This attitude is not too different from that of the Hopi Indians: "A man need not be ashamed of being poor, or of being dumb, so long as he was good to others" (Lee 1959:20). A quick mind is not an asset in itself, but only when used properly. Many Amish believe that what is learned slowly is remembered better. Abraham Lincoln is quoted as saying, "My mind is like a piece of steel—very hard to scratch anything on it, but almost impossible after you get it there, to rub it out." Another Amish motto expresses it this way:

If you would have your learning stay,
  Be patient, don't learn too fast;
The man who travels a mile each day
  May get around the world at last.

Subject grades are given for achievement, not effort. Daily and weekly grades are averaged with test grades to get the score that goes onto the report card. The children know what their daily grades are; in some schools they keep a record of their grades so they can also figure their own averages. A distribution curve that balances B's and D's and gives the majority of children C's is never used by the Amish. Not only are the number of pupils too small but this would lead to an unacceptable type of competition in which one child's good grade would depend on another child's poor grade. They prefer an absolute grading system in which a given number corresponds to a given letter grade. Grades are not manipulated to motivate the student; rather students are taught to accept the level of work they are able to do, to always work hard to do better, to "try, try again," and to remember that "it isn't so bad when you have tried and can't succeed as when you start thinking of giving up before you have really tried." Students are told, "God does not ask for success but for effort." Differences in ability are assessed realistically and accepted matter-of-factly. A mother will say, in front of her children, "This child is an easy learner," and pointing to another, comment, "He learns hard," in much the same way she might comment, "Reuben has blue eyes, Paul's are brown."

Consistent with the oral tradition, Amish children commit a considerable amount of material to memory. They memorize poems and Bible verses the teacher selects. They memorize songs so they can sing while they work and will not be dependent on books. They sing and recite at their Christmas programs. All eight grades in one school that tested unusually high in arithmetic recited in unison the multiplication tables from 2 through 12 and the tables of conversions of measurements, weights, and volumes. The children enjoyed it as they would enjoy choral reading, and it never failed to impress visitors. It was a pleasant way for the children to learn the arithmetic facts, for they did it as a group activity, protected from the embarrassment of obvious error by the carrying capacity of 40 voices. Just as the children memorize hymns and Bible verses before they really understand them, so these children knew their multiplication tables before they used or understood them.

The discussion method is not considered appropriate for academic subjects, for every child is expected to learn the facts and to be able to recite them. Instead of the children wildly waving hands and competing for the chance to answer, each child is questioned by the teacher, each is given a turn to answer, and each child answers the same number of questions. Learning is not disguised as a game. The children are taught that it is work, and although in the Amish culture work is something that must be done whether or not one likes it, whether or not it is convenient, the prevailing attitude is that people are fortunate to be able to work and that work is something to enjoy. "The spirit in happiness is not merely in doing what one likes to do, but to try to like what one has to do."

Discussion is used very effectively in areas where applicable. In many schools the children help to formulate the rules—although the teacher always has veto power—and these are openly and honestly discussed. Sometimes in the public schools the attempt to have a democratic classroom may blur the lines of decision making: the teacher "helps" the children democratically reach the "correct" decision (Jules Henry in Spindler 1963:230). This is not the case in Amish schools. A decision is either made by the teacher, the school board, or the parents, without discussing it with the children who are told what is acceptable. When the children are invited to participate in a decision, however, their opinions are respected and they are actually allowed to reach their own decision. Because Amish schools are homogeneous and there is an emphasis on sensitivity to the group and on the individual working for the good of the group, this effective procedure is good preparation for future participation in church decisions. The larger boundaries are set by the teacher as representative of the community; within these boundaries the children are given freedom of choice. The same is true for the adult church member who within the boundaries set up by the community expresses individual freedom and as an individual member of the church will participate in the formulation and reformulation of the *Ordnung*.

Control is relaxed during recess and the noon hour when the children play vigorously, freely, and noisily. "Play at recess and noon opens our mind for study," said one teacher. Most schools have relatively few rules. One teacher explained, "The only rule really needed is the Golden Rule."

The Amish stress humility, the elimination of self-pride, mutual encouragement, persistence, the willingness to attempt a difficult task, and love for one another. A perusal of mottoes on schoolroom walls, of verses memorized, and of teachers' sayings illustrates the consistency of these values. For the Amish, education is primarily social rather than individual. Its goal is not "the freedom which exalts the individual" (Educational Policies Commission 1962:3), but social cohesion. Teaching the children to get along together in work and play is as important as teaching the academic subjects—both are essential for the continued existence of the Amish community. Specific teaching techniques and hints are mentioned in numerous teachers' letters and articles in the *Blackboard Bulletin*. The book *School*

Bells Ringing, by Uria Byler, discusses methods for teaching every subject from phonics to health and also gives suggestions on such things as playing games, keeping the schoolhouse clean, and dealing with "newspaper pests." Over 80 teachers contributed to the book *Tips for Teachers, A Handbook for Amish Teachers* (Pathway 1970).

In Amish schools the number of pupils per teacher ranges from thirteen to forty-seven, with twenty-seven as the average number. This number keeps the teachers busy. They have worked out a variety of ways for the children to help teach. In some schools the children exchange papers for checking. In other schools the older children help check the papers of the younger children. One teacher has the rule that grades five through eight may not read library books until the arithmetic papers for the lower grades have been corrected and that the third and fourth grades may not have library books until the first and second grade workbooks and arithmetic papers have been corrected. In other schools some of the oldest children may help with reading words, give flash cards to the younger children, or listen to them read. Children also are permitted to help each other. These practices not only reinforce the children's learning by reviewing earlier material, but they also encourage concern and care for the younger children. Helping the teacher in specified ways is consistent with the Amish concept of sharing one another's burdens. However, the teacher must administer the program in such a way that she does not seem to the parents to shirk her leadership responsibility. Some teachers have a paid helper who answers hands. These are often girls who are recent graduates. One teacher explained that her helper is a mother who comes to school three afternoons per week. She takes the lower grades and always has the same subjects. That way she can plan her lessons in advance without asking where they are and what took place in class since.

The Amish teacher is the recognized leader of the classroom, the one who is in charge and responsible. As would be expected, the Amish children identify closely with their teacher. Many of the mottoes and sayings used in the school include the teacher with the pupils:

> As the bird's song is refreshing every morning, so *we* should refresh each other with friendliness.
> Do *we* wonder at times what use *our* little life may be? Well, all that is asked from *us* is to fill *our* little place in this world as best *we* can. This could be a place important or one that is unimportant in the eyes of men. [Italics added.]

Many of the teachers enjoy playing with the children during recess and the noon hour, as much as the children enjoy having them play. The school has the atmosphere of a well-ordered family, in which the teacher represents a parent or an older sibling. The pupils and teacher call one another by their first names, as is done throughout the Amish communities, where even the younger children call the oldest women, the ministers, and the bishops by their first names. Respect is not based on titles.

The teachers plan occasional surprises for their pupils: a picnic in the woods, popcorn at noon, or a special trip. They may even plan a trip for their pupils during the summer. Sometimes a teacher will invite the children to her house for dinner,

Additions or changes can be made to those rules with the approval of all shareholders.

The above has been approved by all shareholders. All parents should have a copy of this and standard booklet.

The above share and tuition rates have changed. The schoolhouse was rebuilt. This increased the share and tuition rates considerably. No shares cost less than what the original shareholders had invested but new share money will be divided among original shareholders, until shares are equal, then share rates will decrease. The treasurer has record of share and tuition rates.

The "School Rules" and "Rules of Conduct for Pupils, Teacher and Parents" emphasize community cooperation and participation of everyone.

Amish teachers from three states were asked, "What, in your opinion, constitutes good control in the schoolroom?" One teacher from Pennsylvania answered, "Good control is wearing a smile, regardless of how you feel inside. Be firm. Have a strong backbone, but not too stiff that is doesn't want to bend when necessary. A teacher should be humble." Another, from Ohio, said, "Be firm, not stern. . . .

School Rules

1. Come in when bell rings and quite down immediately.

2. Do not leave school grounds without permission.

3. Do not take any school property home without permission.

4. Do not play in or around toilets.

5. Stay off the toilet roofs.

6. Do not write on books or any school property.

7. Take good care of all school (and other peoples) property.

8. Do not use bad or unclean language.

9. Do not copy, cheat, or lie.

10. Help along with the singing.

11. Do not talk about, or make fun of, either teacher (or pupils) at any time.

12. Be truthful, Honest, and respectful, <u>always.</u>

13. Whispering, making motions, talking when not ask to talk, attracting attention in any way in school hours is strictly forbidden.

14. A pupil shall not openly correct the teacher of any mistakes at any time.

15. If after a fair warning, these rules are disobeyed, the teacher may expell the pupils involved.

Child may return to school after a called meeting for child's parents, teacher and board of directors.

SIGNED BY BOARD OF DIRECTORS

_____Pres.

_____Sect.

_____Treas.

_____

Rules of conduct for Pupils, Teacher and Parents

RULE 1

CHILDREN   Obey the Teacher in all thing's.
TEACHER   Teacher shall obey Directors.

RULE 2

CHILDREN   When the bell rings go to your seat at once, quietly, do not run in Schoolroom ex-
           cept in an emergency.
TEACHER   Alway's ring the bell on time, then show by example that it means immediate order.

RULE 3

CHILDREN   During School hour s do not whisper, laugh, copy or annoy other's, be quiet.
TEACHER   Keep Children quiet and orderly during School hour's and in good behavior at recess,
           also use enough discipline or pleading to keep order.

RULE 4

CHILDREN   Take good care of your books, pencils and desks; keep your desk neat and tidy.
TEACHER   See that the Children are not careless; keep the School house clean and neat.

RULE 5

CHILDREN   Go to toilet at recess; do not leave your desk during School hours without permission.
Pupils wishing to leave Schoolroom for hygienic purposes shall hold up one hand with two fingers
           unfolded, and only one out at a time.
TEACHER   Do not allow a child to leave its seat during School hours without permission.

RULE 6

CHILDREN   Be kind and friendly to everyone, play the games fair.
TEACHER   Be respectful to each child alike, do not honor one more then another, help them with
           their problems.

RULE 7

CHILDREN   In all things, do nothing unto others that you do not want them to do to you.
TEACHER   Teach the Golden Rule.

RULE 8

CHILDREN   Never go outside Schoolyard fence without permission.
TEACHER   See that the children stay on the Schoolgrounds and allow no unjust playing or rough
           treatment.

RULE 9

CHILDREN   Do not do or say anything you would not do or say in front of Jesus or your parents.
TEACHER   Do not teach anything that is not fit for a Christain Child to know, nor allow reading
           of bad books.

RULE 10

PARENTS   See that your Child is in School on time, teach the Child to honor and obey the Teacher,
and be respectful to everyone; teach the Child to study; and do their work neat; teach the Child to
behave going to and from School, and to respect people they meet. VISIT THE SCHOOL!

Have respect for the pupils, be honest with yourself and admit your mistakes if in the wrong. Be cheerful and slow to anger." Others mentioned trusting the children, not having too many rules, and being careful that no one, including the teacher, breaks them.

This same group of teachers was asked about the methods of discipline they used. The most common form was speaking to the offending child, often in private. Some teachers have the children apologize, but mention that "a false or forced apology is worse than none." A common punishment for a fairly serious offense is keeping children in their seats during recess or the noon hour. Sometimes, in addition, they have to write sentences during this period. Finally, corporal punishment, either a strap across the palm or paddling, may be used. Some teachers never use it; those who do state that it should be used very infrequently and with love. One teacher observed that it is "very effective but should be used with caution and plenty of love. I use it only for lying, cheating, vulgar language, or smutty talk, which is rare." Another teacher said, "We teachers should always see to it that punishing is done out of love. If it isn't, I believe it causes more harm than good, only causing rebellion on the part of the child."

Physical punishment is used for the infractions mentioned above, for open disobedience, and for activity that is physically dangerous, such as children running onto the highway or teasing a nervous buggy horse. Parents approve of limited use of physical punishment to enforce their children's moral and physical safety, but they do not tolerate physical punishment as a substitute for respect or as a means of frightening children into obedience. The occasional teacher who resorts to these methods soon finds himself looking for a different kind of employment.

Teachers use encouragement and rewards much more than punishment. Children are given stars, stickers, even pencils and candy bars for good behavior, good grades, and abiding by the rules. Not all teachers, however, approve of this. One teacher writes, "In my humble opinion, it works better to reward or treat the children unexpectedly, whether at home or at school, for their efforts and good work, *after* the task is done, rather than to promise rewards if they do this or that thing according to our wishes." Another teacher says she always has a treat for her pupils at the end of the six-weeks test day, not just for those who received 100 percent, but for all those who did their best. "Needless to say, no one admits not having done his best," one teacher said. Each one gets a candy bar, a pack of Lifesavers, or some popcorn.

Amish teachers aim never to belittle their pupils or to use sarcasm or ridicule as a means of controlling them. They try to make the children understand their transgressions and accept punishment willingly—because it is deserved. Amish teachers feel emotionally very close to their pupils, and the children in turn admire and want to please their teachers.

RELATION TO PARENTS AND SCHOOL BOARD

There is some tension between the parents and the teacher. Teachers are sensitive to parental criticism. They are especially vulnerable, for a teacher can be criticized not only for what or how she teaches, but how she dresses and spends her free time. The Amish believe very firmly that the training and conversion of children is the responsibility of the parents, not of the school—even an Amish school. The school teaches the child, and to that extent it is an extension of the parents, who have trained him well enough to make him receptive to the teaching he receives in school. The basis of classroom discipline is the respect of the children for the teacher and the teacher's respect for each child and each family. If the parents do not respect the teacher, the children feel this and the teacher soon has serious discipline problems.

The parents express their affection for the teacher in many ways. They bring small gifts of food, they invite the teacher to supper and to spend the night, and they may organize a birthday surprise. Sometimes the parents will get together and make a friendship quilt for the teacher—perhaps with each child's signature embroidered on the family's square. In some of the schools the parents take turns bringing in a hot lunch once a month during the winter for the teacher and children. Unmarried teachers often try to spend at least one night a term in the home of every family in the school.

Parents are urged to visit their schools. Most schools leave it up to the parents' discretion when they should come, but their requests are persuasive. Parents are reminded that they don't put their steers out to pasture and never bother to check on them—and certainly their children are more valuable than cattle. Different schools have worked out various methods to get the parents to visit school regularly. In one school the parents drew dates out of a hat and then visited during their assigned week. In another school the parents decided to visit in order of the age of the father, with one couple coming each week. A teacher in Pennsylvania listed some of the advantages of parents' visiting school, and the disadvantages of their not visiting. Here are the advantages of regular parental visits:

1. Teacher gets an opportunity to visit with the parents.
2. Children get the feeling they (the parents) are a part of the school. It makes them feel important; they are being looked after.
3. The students have brushed up considerably in their lessons. They aren't going to be caught standing in class looking like a dumbbell.
4. Respect in many ways has greatly improved.
5. Teacher has the privilege to discuss discipline problems, if there are any, with the parents.

Here are the disadvantages if parents do not visit school:

1. Teacher has no fellowship with parents.
2. Children become careless; after all, no one is coming in to check on them except the teacher.
3. Children become rude.
4. Teacher has to work doubly hard to keep everyone happy and friendly.
5. Parents cannot understand low report card marks.
6. Discipline problems are hard to overcome.

Many teachers feel that parental visits support the teachers' authority and make the job easier and more pleasant.

Parents come to the school when it is not in session to participate in frolics and work bees, to get the school and yard ready for the new term, to cut and stack wood, to repaint the woodwork, or to refinish the desks.

Many schools have meetings for the parents and board members every month. They strive for 100 percent attendance, but this is of course not possible. Teachers rely on these meetings. Any problems can then be brought up to get some idea of community consensus on what should be done; even if there are no problems, the meetings still serve a worthy function. These are evenings the teachers look forward to and delight in. One teacher says that the fathers trudging through the snow carrying their lanterns "show interest." And an evening together discussing farm sales, wood cutting, manure hauling, and schoolwork is helping to lay a foundation for the future generation.

The teachers look to their school boards for guidance, support, and direction. The school board acts as a buffer between the teacher and the parents, between the teacher and the wider community, when such a buffer is needed. Most teachers say that they take all their problems to the school board: "My board is a great help by seeing that there are plenty of supplies, books, workbooks, especially for the lower grades, paper, pencils, etc." Last but not least important is their visiting the school frequently. It is encouraging when I meet the board members and they have smiles on their faces. "I realize their job is not always the most pleasant, for they have the task of trying to satisfy the [Amish] taxpayers, parents, teachers and probably their wives and themselves," one teacher explained.

Any problems with uncooperative parents or children are taken to the board. Good school board members consider their teacher's happiness. They stop on the way to town to inquire if she needs anything; they often have her over for supper and to spend the night; they may take her to church with them. Members of the school board often function as family for women or single men who are teaching outside their home church district. As is characteristic of the Amish culture, the relationship between the school board members and the school teacher is a personal one.

The school board hires and fires the teacher, woos her, and accepts her resignation. Many teachers seem to feel that it is not good to teach too long in the same school, and some parents believe that it is better if the children have more than one teacher during their years of schooling. A good teacher/board relationship was described by two teachers who said that, though this is their fourth year of teaching in the same school, they are treated as though it were their first. The school board and parents are anxious to have them stay. A problem may arise when a school board says nothing to a teacher about whether or not they want her back in the fall, since it is not the teacher's position to broach the subject unless she plans to leave. Experienced teachers recommend changing schools at least for one year if the teacher feels at all undecided about continuing.

School boards, in conjunction with parents, also make and implement decisions that affect the teachers' personal comforts—decisions to build a house for the teacher, set up a trailer for her, or build outside stairs at the home where she rooms so she can have her own entrance and not have to go through the family kitchen every time she leaves and enters. They must be concerned with all aspects of running the school, and therefore, with their teacher's equipment, living arrangements, and general contentment.

Uria R. Byler (1969) points out that it takes a lot of time and energy to be a good school board member and that those who serve should be "pushers," always working to keep the school going, to improve it, and help start a new school when needed.

What is it like to be a teacher? "It is being a teacher, a guidance counsellor, a policeman, a detective, a judge, a nurse, and a bookkeeper all at one time. It is both exhilarating and frustrating; it is both exalting and humiliating . . . you do all this and receive only a modest salary. But the surprising thing is that most teachers don't envy the factory workers one bit. Give me a classroom with its you-never-know-what-to-expect atmosphere." (*Blackboard Bulletin,* May 1983:1).

6 / The Amish Scholar

Thus far we have described the Amish cultural values, the Amish school, and the Amish teacher. We now turn to the product of Amish schooling. Are Amish "scholars" who graduate from the schools prepared to assume the responsibilities required of their society? Given the Amish educational system, what occupations are the Amish pupils best suited for? What personality characteristics do they possess? How do their academic accomplishments compare to the "English" of similar age and grade level? What are their aspirations and motivations? And what of the Amish drop-out?

In her study of the Pueblos, anthropologist Ruth Benedict (1957) concluded that a basic set of personality traits were common to their society. Their modal personality characteristics, she said, were: "sobriety, moderation, orderliness, and cooperativeness." To what extent do the Amish share homogeneous habit systems and psychological characteristics that conform to a type? We shall discuss the Amish modal personality. But first, we shall describe their academic achievements on standardized tests.

STANDARDIZED TEST RESULTS

How do Amish achievement scores compare to the "English"? We used as a control group, pupils from rural public schools, and we chose achievement tests that were appropriate and generally considered reliable. We gave the tests to Amish scholars in several different cultural settings: those Amish who were in Amish-run schools, those who attended all-Amish public schools, and those who attended integrated (Amish and non-Amish in about equal proportions) public schools. The technical research findings are discussed in greater detail in the research report (Hostetler 1969:43–54) and in a dissertation by Wayne Miller (1969).

SRA Tests of Educational Ability. The average composite score for language, reasoning, and quantitative ability for the eighth-grade Amish was 96.7 and for the non-Amish, 99.5, a difference that was not statistically significant. The scores showed no significant difference between the Amish in their own schools, those in all-Amish public schools, or those integrated in public schools.

The Amish children scored significantly lower in the language section of the IQ test than did the control group. Although the Amish pupils scored higher than the non-Amish in the sections on reasoning and quantitative ability, the difference was not significant.

Iowa Tests of Basic Skills.   Six of the eleven possible testing areas were administered: vocabulary, reading comprehension, spelling, English grammatical word usage, knowledge and use of reference materials, and arithmetic problem solving. When scores of the Amish and rural public school children were compared by subject matter, the Amish excelled in spelling, word usage, and arithmetic. These differences are statistically significant in favor of the Amish.

The non-Amish control group overtook the Amish in vocabulary. In use of reference material and reading comprehension, the two groups were virtually equal. In other words, only in [English] vocabulary did the non-Amish children out-perform the Amish children. There were no significant differences in the Iowa achievement scores between the Amish in public schools and those in Amish schools except in the area of word usage. The students in Amish schools did significantly better in word usage than did the Amish students in public schools. The composite achievement scores for all skills tested ranked by group from high to low in this order: Amish pupils in Amish schools, Amish in all-Amish public schools, and Amish pupils in public schools with non-Amish children. This pattern of achievement on the Iowa Tests of Basic Skills attests to the adequacy of the Amish schools.

The generally low performance of the Amish on the language aspects of the two tests described above can perhaps be attributed in part to the time limitation. On rechecking the reading tests we found that the children did very well in the parts they finished; but, especially in the upper grades, most of the children who had not been trained to take timed tests did not complete the work. It should also be remembered that English is a second language that is not learned until they enter school.

Amish parochial students taking the Canadian Tests of Basic Skills in 1989 tested highest in word usage, spelling and arithmetic computations—five to seven months above the national grade equivalent, and lowest—six and seven months below grade equivalent—in mathematical concepts and visual materials, which involve interpreting maps, graphs and tables. The composite scores for all students in all categories was just above grade. In 1987 the Iowa Tests of Basic Skills were given to 197 Amish parochial school children in grades three through eight. All sections were given except science and social studies. The students tested above grade level in every category except English vocabulary which fell slightly below grade equivalency but never below the average national stanine of 4.5. The students tested highest in mathematical computation and word usage and were at or above grade in all total scores: reading, language skills, work skills and mathematical skills. At every grade level the pupils tested above grade in the total composite scores with the eighth grade testing almost a full grade higher. The composite scores for an additional 117 Amish parochial students tested in 1988 measured at or above grade level for every grade.

These standardized test results indicate that the Amish parochial schools, now taught by teachers educated in Amish schools, are continuing to give their students an adequate academic education, even when judged by measures designed to test students in our modern, technological society. Amish parochial schools are prepar-ing their students for successful, responsible adulthood within their own culture and within the larger society.

Stanford Achievement Test.   For comparison we obtained from public school records the Stanford Achievement Test scores for Amish and non-Amish pupils in a large geographic area in the Midwest. Scores were available for the first six grades. The Amish and non-Amish scores were about equal in most areas; however, here too, the Amish made slightly higher scores in arithmetic than did the non-Amish.

Some Amish teachers have shown interest in giving standardized tests in their schools regularly for the past few years. The level of achievement on these tests (Iowa Tests of Basic Skills and the Canadian Tests of Basic Skills) in Iowa, Indiana, Ontario, and other places show satisfactory performance. In the state of Iowa, Amish schools are required to administer achievement tests annually to apply for exemption from state statutes requiring teacher certification.

Draw-a-Man Test.   (The Goodenough-Harris Draw-a-Man Test, Harris: 1963.) This test was chosen to measure nonverbal intelligence. In addition to measuring intelligence, the test provides insights into cultural influences, ability to form concepts, and ability to conceptualize relationships. It has been widely used, as Harris (1964) reports, in nonliterate cultures. The test requires the pupil to draw a man, a woman, and himself. The man drawings were scored, using 100 as a mean standard IQ measure.

The test was given to 389 pupils between the ages of six and fifteen in Amish schools, and the results were compared to U.S. norms. Only the drawings of a man have been validated as an indicator of intelligence. We used the drawings of a woman and of self to gain additional insights into cultural factors. The Amish pupils in twelve Amish schools had a combined intelligence score of 101.6. The twelve schools ranged from a low 91.5 to a high of 112.7. The achievement in this test in the various Amish schools paralleled the degree of taboo against representing the human figure in the various communities. In spite of this taboo, pupils in Amish schools scored from 4.3 to 10.3 points higher than those Amish who attended public schools.

Whether the human figure was drawn with Amish or non-Amish characteristics presumably made no difference in the scores. An analysis of the drawings for such cultural influences, however, proved interesting. Differences were found between the drawings of the sexes. Amish boys in public school drew English-like (non-Amish) persons more frequently than did the girls. Amish girls were much more reserved in the use of English features in their drawing of the human figure. This difference in the sexes is consistent with what we know about the acculturation patterns in Amish culture, namely, that men are more exposed to, and are probably more at ease in, the outer world than are women. Pupils in Amish schools drew persons in Amish dress far more than did Amish pupils who attended public school. Occasionally an Amish child in public school would even draw himself as non-Amish. The drawings from the Amish schools clearly reflect the traditional culture. Amish pupils in public schools identify more with English or alien role models and values than the children in the Amish schools.

Cultural factors in the use of tests.   Amish attitudes toward testing, we found, vary among schools and communities. Some schools permitted testing but did not wish to have the children draw the human figure in the Draw-a-Man test. Their objection was part of the general taboo against photography and representation of the human figure. Attitudes toward testing also varied with the experience and training of the teacher. Interest in standardized testing generally was shown by those teachers who had taught for a long time and who were secure in their role in relation to their school board and their community. But some still felt that, in the long run, testing may be harmful to the Amish, even if it is done by sympathetic outsiders.

Only after investing large amounts of time with school board members and teachers was it possible to obtain the cooperation of a sufficient number of schools. It was necessary for our staff to go over the tests themselves, often item by item, with school board members. In one community two years elapsed between the time the tests were explained and the time when consent was obtained. Most parents were not interested in comparing their children's achievement scores to scores of other children in the United States. The notion that the usefulness of the individual is related to a test score is foreign to the Amish, for they believe that each individual has a God-given role in this world. They reject occupations in science, industry, the military, and government.

Amish teachers give periodic tests in the basic subjects they teach. Speed, however, is not stressed in Amish schools. Children are admonished to do careful, accurate work. It is considered better to do what one does well, rather than to do a great deal and make careless mistakes. The pupils are taught not to skip material they do not understand, but to work at it until they have mastered it. The Amish always give their own tests without time limits, for they do not want the children to hurry. Amish children who attend public school often complain, "They never let me finish anything." The Amish child in such a setting works under a heavy disadvantage, since he loses his sense of continuity, expression, and personal fulfillment. This difference in time orientation places Amish children at a disadvantage when taking standardized tests. Instead of learning to work quickly, guess intelligently, and skip those questions they do not understand, the Amish children are taught: "Do not rush over your work in school or at home." "Take your time when making important decisions." "People who are always in a hurry seemingly get very little satisfaction out of life." The children are cautioned not to be "like the world," but to "be contented, and do not worry or try to follow up the world's uneasiness and speed." "Look up into the branches of the trees, knowing that they grew great and strong because they grew slowly and well."

Our design for testing achievement patterns took into account academic subjects that were important to Amish cultural goals. We were interested in assessing educational goals in the context of intercultural relations. Our interest was in subjects the Amish mastered well. The schools we included in the study had in most cases been in existence for two or more years. The teachers were experienced, having taught no less than three years; they were considered by the community to be good teachers. In addition to testing the pupils in these schools, we also observed many other schools in different communities. Since reading, writing, and arithmetic are important in Amish educational goals, we chose tests for these areas, covering vocabulary, reading comprehension, spelling, English grammatical word usage, and ability to solve practical problems. Most Amish schools have limited library facilities. We were interested in how this affected the ability to use reference material, so we gave a test in this area. We also gave a standardized test in the use of reasoning techniques and one on general intelligence. In addition we gave the pupils a nonverbal test of intelligence.

Our aim was to compare Amish schoolchildren objectively with children who attended public schools. We compared Amish schools having noncertified teachers with public schools having all eight grades. Because of their limited access to mass media and because of the use of English as a second language, we anticipated that the Amish would score lower than the non-Amish children in public school, but we were mistaken.

THE AMISH PERSONALITY

There is strong support for the proposition that Amish personality is shaped by their social milieu, that Amish child training and education as described in earlier chapters, points to a "psychic unity." The empirical evidence from the achievement patterns shows clearly that the Amish performance on standardized tests is equal to the "English." But the evidence for a homogeneous personality pattern is based largely on other considerations—the Myers-Briggs Type Indicator, freehand drawings, and vocational preferences.

The Myers-Briggs Type Indicator.   This instrument, based on Jung's personality theory, is used widely in industry and by placement services to match individual skills with occupations most suited to personal style and capability. This indicator is designed to ascertain a person's basic preference pattern in regard to perception and judgment. A person may reasonably be expected to develop most skill with the processes he or she prefers to use and in the areas of a person's interests. The items in the test offer forced choices between given alternatives. A typical question might be: "Would you rather work under someone who is (a) always kind or (b) always fair?" A person's personality type is determined by a letter combination derived from 4 basic indexes:

EI Extraversion or Introversion
SN Sensing or Intuition
TF Thinking or Feeling
JP Judgment or Perception

An individual's type is expressed in a four-letter combination such as ENTP (Extraverted, Intuitive, Thinking, Perceptive). For example, the EI index is designed to reflect whether the person is predominantly an extravert or an introvert, whether he is oriented to the world of people and things or to the inner world of concepts and ideas, and so forth.

The most dominant type to emerge among the Amish children in our samples was ISFJ (Introverted, Sensing, Feeling, Judgmental). Almost thirty percent of the Amish were of this type, as compared to only 6.4 percent of the non-Amish in our sample. But twenty-four percent of the Amish were ESFJ. Thus fifty-four percent of the Amish were SFJ. This degree of homogeneity of personality type is overwhelming and differs from national samples and from the non-Amish children we tested.

Whether in their own schools or in public schools, the Amish showed the same pronounced type. A description of the ISFJ type reads:

> Quiet, friendly, responsible and conscientious. Works devotedly to meet his obligations and serve his friends and school. Thorough and painstaking, accurate with figures but needs time to master technical subjects, as reasoning is not his strong point. Patient with detail and routine. Loyal, considerate, concerned with how other people feel even when they are in the wrong. (Myers 1962:70)

This characterization matches our observations of Amish behavior patterns. No observational data could yield a better description of Amish personality characteristics. According to the results, the Amish personality configurations are least like those of science students and research scientists. The Amish have a very high percentage of Sensing-Feeling preferences, approaching those of sales and customer relations employees (Myers 1980). The test predicts that the Amish personality type will find most satisfaction in occupations requiring dependability, tact, sympathy, hard work, and systematic approach to work. The type harmonizes with Amish cultural themes and values stressed in their society. There was little difference between the response patterns of Amish girls and boys. The four indicators in greater detail read as follows:

The *introvert* likes quietness and concentration in preference to variety and distraction, tends to be careful with detail, prefers not to work fast with complicated procedures, and does not mind working on one project for a long time without interruption. These tendencies contrast with those of the *extravert,* who tends to be impatient with long, slow jobs and is interested in the idea behind the job rather than in how other people do the job. The introvert works well alone and tends to dislike generalities.

The *sensing* type dislikes new problems unless they can be solved in standard ways. He prefers an established routine, enjoys using skills he has already acquired, and works more steadily than the *intuitive* type, who may work in bursts of energy powered with enthusiasm. The sensing type becomes impatient when the details are too complicated to remember. He seldom makes errors of fact and tends to be good at precise work.

The *feeling* type tends to be very aware of other people and of feelings and likes to please people or help them, whereas the *thinking* type may hurt people's feelings without knowing it. The feeling type likes harmony in contrast to analysis, and his efficiency may be badly disturbed by feuds. He dislikes telling people unpleasant things; he finds it difficult to reprimand people or to fire them even when necessary. He is sympathetic, needs people around him, and relates well to most people.

The *judging* type likes to plan his work and finish it on schedule rather than adapt to changing situations. He does not have trouble making decisions but may decide things too quickly. Unlike the *perceptive* type, who likes to work rapidly with complicated tasks, he does not like to start many projects at the same time. He may tend to overlook new things that need to be done. He tends to be satisfied with a judgment on a thing, situation, or person once it is reached.

Many of these characteristics correspond to the values stressed in Amish culture. Respect for others, consideration, helpfulness, sympathy, and even pacifism correspond with the strong *feeling* component of the test, particularly the notion of being "concerned with how other people feel even when they are in the wrong." Such personality endowments help explain why the Amish can be so steady in their work and so steadfast in their faith and how they can adhere so faithfully to the *Ordnung*. These preferences and personality patterns, which the Amish exhibit as children, remain with them as they become adults.

In order to supplement these findings we asked the Amish (and the control group) to make two drawings and to indicate their vocational preferences.

Freehand drawings. Children were instructed to draw "Your home—the home in which you live" and "My happy time—what you do that you enjoy." Children's drawings reveal many aspects of personality, especially how the child views his environment and himself. The drawings of Amish and non-Amish were compared to ascertain whether their themes varied and whether their content was consistent with the value orientations of the children's respective cultures.

Happy-time drawings. The two cultures exhibited some striking differences. The Amish happy-time drawings included work-related activities, whereas the non-Amish drawings contained not a single work-related drawing. Amish work-related activity included such tasks as baby-sitting, raking leaves, gathering eggs, and baking. These activities are obviously important in the lives of the Amish children, for they perform such duties as part of the routine of living on the farm. Non-Amish children are probably given fewer assigned tasks and their participation in work is less important to the functioning of the household than in the Amish home. Certainly such tasks are not associated with happiness. Other Amish happy-time drawings depicted reading, eating, sledding, fishing, ice-skating, playing ball, swinging, hunting, and going on a trip.

The non-Amish happy-time drawings showed marked competitive activity and some hostility. They included watching television, swimming, snowball fights, hitting the teacher with a snowball, throwing an object at an automobile, playing basketball, buying new things at the store, wrestling with the dog, and "blowing up the school."

The Amish included others in their drawings to a much greater extent than did the non-Amish. Being with others is apparently important to Amish children, and when they draw pictures of a happy time, they see themselves as part of a group. Their drawings appear less individualistic than the non-Amish drawings.

More frequently than the non-Amish the Amish children included outdoor activity in their drawings. Amish boys showed a greater preference for outdoor activity than did Amish girls, which is consistent with Amish adult roles. Non-Amish children do not aspire to be farmers or to work outdoors and their drawings show more indoor activity than the Amish drawings. The Amish boys depicted activities somewhat different from those depicted by Amish girls, but these differences were not as great as between the non-Amish boys and girls. Amish male activities are related to the adult male role in the farm environment, but many Amish girls also prefer such male-related activities as fishing or working with animals. The absence of a strong differentiation of activities between the sexes suggests that, at least for elementary school age, the Amish have no rigid dichotomy between male and female concepts of "a happy time."

Man   Woman   Self

Drawing by girl age 10.

Man   Woman   Self

Drawing by girl age 13.

Man   Woman   Self

Drawing by boy age 14.

The Goodenough-Harris Draw-A-Man Test. Top: Drawings by a child attending an Amish school reflect traditional Amish values and patterns. Middle and Bottom: Drawings by Amish children in public schools. Amish children who attend public school identify more with "alien" values than do children who attend Amish schools.

House drawings. Amish drawings include large farmhouses, often with a variety of color and many windows, and other features of the farm environment—such as porches on the house, walks, gardens, roads, and even mudholes. The drawings reflect regional aspects of Amish culture, so that those of us who knew the several communities could tell from the style of the architecture or landscape in the drawing whether the drawing came from a community in Ohio, Indiana, or Pennsylvania.

The children were instructed to "write something about your house if you wish." Amish children wrote comments such as: "This is the house where I live," "I like my home," "I like to work in my house and barn." They had positive feelings about their homes. Many of their drawings included other dwellings or objects—a barn, sidewalks, or a garden—which they thought of as part of the home. In contrast the non-Amish children rarely drew surrounding buildings and sometimes drew only their own bedroom or a single room in the dwelling. Amish children learn that "home is not a place to go when there is no other place to be, but the center of all good things." The Amish children's use of color differed greatly from one school to another. They used green and blue, but they also made liberal use of red, yellow, and brown.

Regulation and conformity, rather than spontaneity, are dominant characteristics in their drawings, as was also observed in fieldwork. The drawings indicate that rule is important in the life of both Amish boys and girls. These drawings show some of the dominant Amish personality characteristics, interests, self-conceptions, and patterns of interaction with the environment. The Amish children depict their external environment at an unusually early age. They use color realistically from the age of six. They are able to make spatial relationships at an early age, an important indication of social growth and socialization. The deemphasis of the self and the importance of the group (family and community) show that the Amish child is responding at a very young age to the external environment and the value patterns of Amish culture, which emphasize the family and the church-community, not the individual. External rather than subjective elements seem dominant in the drawings.

Vocational preferences. Personality characteristics are revealed by attitudes toward work and by vocational interests. Amish children were asked to write a short theme on the topic, "What kind of work I want to do when I grow up, and why," and to give their age, sex, and their father's occupation. This method of investigation, used by Goodman (1957) and by Freed and Freed (1968), reveals not only vocational aspirations, but also the extent of continuity of interests between the old and the young.

Responses were obtained from Amish and non-Amish groups of children. The Amish children were from both traditional communities in densely populated settlements and from communities that were relaxed with respect to the older traditions. Some of the less-traditional schools were in small settlements or were geographically marginal to the larger communities. The 242 Amish responses were grouped into "traditional" and "nontraditional" Amish vocations and the vocational preferences were compared to their father's occupation.

The pupils in the traditional communities generally chose vocations in keeping with the Amish values. They were farm-related and included trades associated with the Amish way of life: carpentry, harness-making, blacksmithing, working in a carriage repair shop, sawmilling, logging, woodworking, and often a choice of farming combined with another occupation. A few responses representative of those that followed the traditional vocational pattern are these:

An Amish boy, 9 years old, wrote:

When I grow up I want to be a good farmer. Because I like to milk and feed the pigs, chickens, horses, cows, and calves. Also I get the straw and hay down. . . . Father teaches me to farm.

An Amish boy, 13 years old and in the eighth grade, wrote:

I want to be a farmer and this is why. I like farming because I like to get up early in the morning and do the chores. When I have eaten I like to go out in the fields and plow or disk or whatever needs to be done. When I need a tool shed to put my tools in, I would build a building because I like to hammer nails. When I would break something I would go to town and buy a new part, or if I had a welder I would weld it. When it is time to make hay I would try to get my neighbors to help and would bring the hay in after dark when it is nice and cool.

A girl, age 13, wrote:

When I grow up I want to be a housekeeper, bake, cook, iron, wash, and have a garden. I don't want to live in the city. I would have a few flower beds in the lawn so it wouldn't look so bare. I want to be a housekeeper, because my mother taught me how to cook. I want to have a garden so I wouldn't have to buy the vegetables and things. I don't want to live in the city so that I wouldn't have to hear all the noise. I want to work out, to help people.

A school-age boy works in the same field as his grandfather, preparing the soil for planting corn. (Photo by Richard Reinhold.)

An Amish girl in her last year of elementary school explains what she hopes to do when she becomes an adult:

> I would want to live on a farm and keep house. I would want to bake, sew, cook, wash clothes, iron, make Christmas candy to sell, knit mufflers, and many other things. I would want a lawn to mow, trim, and rake. I would have very nice flowers all around the house. I would bake bread and rolls. I'd make patty's and doughnuts ever so good. I'd make noodles too.
>
> I would live on a farm too so I'd always have lots of work. I'd help milk cows, feed a dog, a dozen cats and kittens and the chickens, too, so I don't have to buy eggs. I'd help in the fields and put hay in. I would help other neighbors too with their work, so when I need help they'll help me too. I would spend a day at my parents, brothers, or sisters places too. I think I'd find time to visit at Sam Yoder's school one afternoon.
>
> The reason why I'd want to live on a farm and keep house is because there are always so many interesting things to do which I enjoy.

These children look forward with happy anticipation to the roles they will fill as adults.

Those occupational choices that ordinarily cannot be carried out on the family farm were grouped as nontraditional. They included working in a restaurant, working in a factory, nursing, teaching, being an editor, managing a bookstore, and being a cowboy. The vocation of teacher is difficult to classify, since this role is emerging as an acceptable one in Amish society. It is presently regarded as a calling rather than a form of making a living. The following responses written by Amish children are representative of nontraditional vocations:

A boy, age 8, wrote:

> When I grow up I would like to be a fire chief of a town whose population would be about 8,000. I would want to drive a big fire truck. The reason I want to be a fire chief is because I could give orders. I also like to go to fires, or maybe I could rescue somebody.

A boy, age 13, wrote:

> I would like to be a man that handles books a lot. A librarian, a secretary, or anything that has to do with books. I like almost any kind of books but I prefer Westerns and mystery books. Since my mother was also a bookworm I guess I got the love of books from her. Anyway in my spare time I want a book in my hands.

A boy in grade 2, age 7, wrote:

> I want to be an auctioneer. I like to shout.

A girl in her last year of elementary school, age 13, wrote:

> When I grow up I want to be a waitress in a restaurant. I have always wanted to wait on people. But I have never thought of being a waitress till lately. I would like to work six days a week, Monday till Saturday. I think it would be fun to wait on people, because then I would meet other people. But I would want to come home every evening.

Such responses came from Amish schools that were marginal with respect to traditional Amish customs. Yet each of the nontraditional vocational choices was a service occupation and each reflected parental preferences and love of work. It would appear that even when Amish children choose marginal occupations, the general value pattern of the culture is maintained. The choices are consistent with rather than antagonistic to the Amish value orientation.

In a public school with a student population composed of approximately one-third Amish and two-thirds non-Amish, the Amish children responded very differently from their non-Amish schoolmates. The dominant choice of the Amish boys was farming, with many specifying dairy farming, hog raising, horse farming, or simply, "I wish to be a farmer." In one school where there were 28 Amish boys, 18 wished to be farmers. Of 38 non-Amish boys in the same school, only 3 chose farming as an occupation. Other non-Amish choices fell into the professional category: scientists, government service, astronaut, artist, and leader in sports. Amish girls in public schools showed a marked preference for service-oriented vocations, such as teaching and nursing. Their other choices were in the category of unskilled manual labor, such as housekeeping: "be a housewife," "work at somebody else's house," "cleaning house, taking care of the children and cooking." The non-Amish girls preferred such vocations as secretary, actress, modeling; none preferred a vocation that could be classed as unskilled manual labor.

Clearly Amish children have a concept or value pattern for vocation different from that of non-Amish children. They see and are taught that their fathers hold their jobs because of an "Amish way of life." They emulate the occupations of their fathers and mothers and sense no stigma attached to aspiring toward such a role. They know through participation in adult activities that they can fulfill their aspirations when they become adults. The children in the Old Order Amish community know what they want to do; they know what they will be doing when they become adults; and they are receiving the emotional, psychological, and technical training essential for productive adulthood as Amish men and women.

Smucker (1988:227–31) reported that Amish children rated their families more positively than non-Amish children, and suggested that the "identity" crisis among the Amish is resolved earlier in life than among the non-Amish. The Amish children manifested less feeling of hostility and aggression. The Amish, he points out, know exactly what to expect and what is expected of them as they enter the adult world. At approximately the same time that the non-Amish children are coping with an emerging self, the Amish children have already accepted the limited role of the self in their culture.

DROPOUTS FROM AMISH SOCIETY

What happens to the Amish child who does not wish to terminate his education with the Amish system? The answer is very simple. Any child who continues his schooling into high school, either immediately after completing the eighth grade or later, will not remain Amish. It is extremely rare for a child who has attended Amish schools to enter high school. This may occur if his family changes church affiliations by joining a liberalized group. A few Amish pursue higher education in their late teens or after the age of 21 by taking correspondence courses. The number of such persons is decidedly limited. Such persons usually choose to become nurses or teachers, bookkeepers, or professions that are least objectionable and that will be useful to the Amish community. Sometimes individuals will take "trade courses," such as upholstery, by correspondence. An insatiable desire for learning is manifest in a few.

Amish persons who pursue higher education usually come from families who themselves are liberal or atypical in some way. The parents may be lenient in respect to the rules of the community, or perhaps one of them has secretly nursed the aspiration to follow a profession outside of the Amish pattern, as a teacher, businessman, or missionary, for example. Such unfulfilled aspirations of parents may be sensed by the young and accepted by them as their own life goals. If families are both large and somewhat marginal to the Amish discipline, the young are less likely to find meaningful work satisfaction on the family farm.

By typical American standards the Amish children are all dropouts, because they do not enter high school. But from the Amish point of view, the Amish child who continues his training through high school and college is a dropout from the Amish religion and way of life. Lack of formal training, however, is no problem for the Amish in obtaining employment in the community. In most settlements where the Amish live, their skills as maids, baby-sitters, housecleaners, seamstresses, laborers, farm tenants, carpenters, builders, and factory workers are sought by the non-Amish people. Many small industries would rather hire an Amish person with only an elementary education than high school graduates, who they say are less likely to be dependable and prompt and are less inclined to give a full day's work. The Amish will not work in unionized plants, however.

There is little foundation to the notion advanced by some that the Amish should be forced to take more years of schooling so that in case they should leave the faith, they would not be disadvantaged educationally. Individuals of Amish background who decide to obtain a higher education are generally highly motivated and capable of doing so. As in any minority group some Amish individuals have personal problems due to culture change and conflict, but these persons do not become a burden on society or welfare recipients.

During periods of military conscription, Amish young men were assigned to alternative service work, often serving as orderlies or employees in city hospitals. Some of these young men turned worldly and occasionally they married nurses. Some who returned to their home communities found life too circumscribed but others became community leaders. Those who married outsiders frequently did not return to their home communities. The threat of losing young men in this manner was solved when Selective Service agreed to assign the young men to farm service.

The economic changes and the pressures of modernity are keenly felt by Amish families. Quilts and other crafts are made in homes and marketed in nearby village stores. As farms become less available and less affordable, the number of Amish who work in industry is increasing. Off-the-farm employment in building and construction trades, factories, markets, and restaurants may trigger significant psychological changes. Already school teachers have observed that children from non-farm Amish families are more defiant, rebellious, and more self-centered than those from farm families (Smucker 1988:231). This trend may result in more role-confusion and instability about who they are and what their future is in the Amish community.

Young people of more liberalized affiliations of Amish, who have adopted modern technology and travel but who have limited sophistication for coping with the problems these innovations can entail, may feel a greater degree of stress and uncertainty than the Old Order youth. We have not included such groups in the scope of this study. The Old Order Amish children genuinely aspire to do the things their parents are doing. They are not impoverished by their own social institutions, nor are they denied emotional or actual participation in their society.

SUMMARY

The Amish personality type may be described as quiet, responsible, and conscientious. The Amish individual works devotedly to meet obligations, and although careful with detail, needs time to master technical subjects. Amish people are not especially good at working rapidly with complicated tasks. They like to do things well. They like an established way of doing things. The Amish modal personality is loyal, considerate, sympathetic. He or she is concerned with how other people feel, even when they are in the wrong. An Amish person dislikes telling people unpleasant things. These personality endowments correspond generally with the values stressed in Amish culture and taught in Amish schools.

Amish children tend to be very aware of other people, they prefer a certain amount of routine, and they relate well to most people. Their drawings reveal preferences for work-related activities; they do not make a sharp distinction between what is work and what is play. Happy-time activities reveal no rigid differentiation between the sexes. Drawings of the Amish home, as the children see it, include a variety of colors, often several buildings, and a spatial orientation of the farm environment that includes roads, gardens, and fences. The drawings reveal a realistic sense of environment, an ability to conceptualize space at an early age, and a strong identification of the individual with the home. The inclusion of others in their drawings suggests the importance of family and group activities.

The vocational aspirations of Amish children are for service occupations and manual work. The children emulate the work roles of adults. Amish boys generally prefer farming or farm-related work. Girls prefer housekeeping, gardening, cooking, cleaning, caring for children, or some type of service, such as nursing or teaching. Their vocational aspirations are realistic and attainable within the limits of Amish culture. As judged by educational testing standards the overall performance of the Amish is similar to that of a representative sample of rural school children in the United States. In spite of the limited exposure the Amish children have to radio, television, and modern school facilities and although the Amish teachers themselves have had only an eighth-grade education, the Amish pupils scored significantly higher in spelling, word usage, and arithmetic than the pupils in our sample of rural public schools. They scored slightly above the national norm in these subjects. In spite of small libraries and limited equipment, the Amish pupils were equal to the non-Amish pupils in comprehension and in the use of reference material. They scored lowest in vocabulary. (No tests were given in German vocabulary.)

In those aspects of learning stressed by the Amish culture, the Amish pupils outperformed pupils in the control group. These findings are suggestive rather than conclusive. The Amish culture provides an environment for its children that is rather sharply delineated from the social climate of our Western civilization. By outside standards this environment is limiting and restricting, but it is multi-dimensional, involving much more than books or video cassettes. Along with the intellectual limits the child acquires a knowledge of what is expected. Learning is directed toward conformity with a knowledge of what is right, rather than toward questioning existing knowledge or discovering new knowledge.

It should be remembered that no one can better judge what is good for the Amish community than the Amish themselves. Any effort to increase creativity or raise performance on standardized school tests among the Amish cannot be undertaken without also introducing the risk of cultural discontinuities. The introduction of greater competitive goals, resulting in greater appeal to self-interest and to self-importance, can only mean in Amish terms the loss of "humility, simple living, and resignation to the will of God."

7 / Perspectives On Amish Education

SCHOOLS AND COMMUNITY: A SINGLE INTEGRATED STRUCTURE

When the Old Order Amish withdrew from the public school system and set up their own schools, state officials believed that it would be impossible for them to give their children an adequate education. The schools were small, with limited equipment; neither their teachers nor their school board members had been graduated from high school; and the schools were completely financed and administered by the local Amish community. Is adequate education possible under such circumstances? In our field work we studied the total Amish culture—the community, the family, and the school—and then selected a sample of Amish schools in various communities in North America for intensive study. One of the criteria for school selection was that the teacher should be experienced, having taught not less than three years, and be considered a good teacher by the Amish community. We concluded that these Amish community schools are successful when judged by public school standards (standardized tests), when judged by independent school certification standards (goal attainment), and when judged by the traditional Old Order Amish community.

The Amish schools are more successful than specialized government schools for minority groups (such as the schools on Indian reservations), where local cultures contribute little to the school and are not identified with the educational system. Amish schools are more successful than many ghetto schools in which middle-class culture rather than the children's experiences determines teachers' attitudes and techniques. They are more successful for Amish children than consolidated schools, for they enable the Amish children not only to master the requisite academic material, but also to develop a positive self-image within their own culture and at the same time to identify with American culture without emulating its total likeness.

Although the Amish schools are admirably suited to the needs of the Amish children and similar schooling might be utilized by other groups within our society, Amish-type schools could not meet the needs of major segments of the population in the United States. By design, Amish schools are not suited for training artists, musicians, painters, and actors; nor for training science-oriented individuals who would pursue engineering, astronomy, paleontology, chemistry, or space technology; nor for training business executives, corporation managers, or occupations leading to government or military careers. The Amish school, by intent, does not function as an institution for upward mobility in the modern industrial complex.

LOCAL CONTROL

For many years the Amish sent their children to the public schools. They established their own schools when they were threatened by the mono-cultural public school that in essence would not grant them an identity of their own and would not permit them to be raised both as Amishmen and as Americans. As long as the public schools were small in size and on a human rather than an organizational scale— therefore local in character—the Amish exerted an influence in the public school as had the Swedes and Finns in other localities. As the administrative unit became larger through consolidation, small, culturally divergent groups were subordinated to the larger numbers of middle-class Americans and thereby lost their influence over the style, as well as the policies, of the schools that serve their children. Today most public schools are controlled by the middle class and reflect that culture regardless of the cultural composition of the students attending any particular school.

Where the Amish were successful in their attempt to modify the public school system, their children remained in the public school and thus continued to be taught by state-certified teachers. They were in an educational situation in which their distinctive culture was respected while they were at the same time introduced to aspects of middle-class American society. Where the state school officials remained rigid and made little attempt to understand or work with the Amish, the Amish withdrew completely from the public schools and built and staffed their own schools. They withdrew because of changes in public school philosophy and organization that threatened their cultural identity, not because they wanted to teach more religion in the school. By Amish standards the public schools had become intolerable for their children. In a similar response, although the specifics of the situation were admittedly very different, some elements of the African-American community tried to make decisions about what could and could not be tolerated for their children in terms of public schooling. Other culture groups such as the Chinese, Japanese, and Jews have for generations countered the public schools by establishing supplementary schools to teach their language and culture to their children.

The Old Order Amish have demonstrated that not only are they able to make a substantial contribution to policy-making in local public schools when they are permitted to, but they can, when necessary, organize and staff their own schools without any outside help despite discouraging legal suits initiated by the state. Our findings indicate that the Amish children in their own schools tested slightly (though not significantly) higher on achievement tests than those who were attending public schools. Perhaps the public school system could be improved by respecting cultural differences and encouraging members of minority groups to participate in the organization and implementation of their children's schooling.

Our study illustrates that local control (in this case complete local control) with no funds or supplies from the government can work well even though the parents have a limited educational background (eight years of formal schooling), speak English as a second language, and are culturally different from the prevailing American culture. By "work well" we mean that the parents are satisfied with the schools, the children who graduate from them are well prepared for adult life, and, as judged by public school standards of success on standardized tests, the children are adequately taught.

EDUCATION FOR COHESION AND CARING

Education for social cohesion and education for technological competence are both essential. We do not want to produce, in Justice Robert Jackson's words, "technically competent barbarians." Nor can we afford to neglect the technical training that is essential if human resources and the resources of the environment are to be utilized in such a manner as to provide a good life for successive generations. If social cohesion is to be developed organically and not imposed by a master technology, then certain educational methods seem to be applicable. For example, in teaching technical competence, the subject matter is the controlling influence, rather than the style of life of the teacher or the students' personal relation to the teacher. An extremely asocial and difficult genius might contribute more technical know-how than a number of intuitive and gifted teachers, but more than the facts are necessary to motivate people to want to live in a style that is not just socially acceptable but is socially responsible.

The Amish stress social responsibility in the education of their children. Social cohesiveness rather than intellectual creativity or critical analysis is the goal of Amish schooling. Therefore, in Amish schools the emphasis on values generally supersedes the emphasis on facts. However, factual material, though somewhat circumscribed, is learned thoroughly. Amish children are taught both by practice and by example to care for and support the members of the school and the community. Under teacher supervision children teach one another within the same grade and across grades.

The Amish are not committed to the assumption that legitimate forms of learning are primarily abstract and analytical. They believe that learning should be practical and should lead to a disciplined life on earth, concern for others, and an eternity in heaven. "The goal of the Old Order Amish Parochial Schools is to prepare for usefulness by preparing for eternity." (*Guidelines,* 1981) In their educational program they utilize drill and rote learning that will lead to shared knowledge and social success.

In addition to the Amish there are other ethnic and linguistic communities whose culture is primarily oral rather than literary, interpersonal rather than impersonal, relationally oriented rather than analytically oriented. Our study of Amish socialization, supported by the results of the Myers-Briggs Type Indicator, clearly suggests the ineptness of preparing these children for analytically related vocations. We suspect that the same would be true of other cultures of the oral-tradition type. The extraordinarily high scores of the Amish in the area of sensing and feeling are consistent with their ability to relate to others, with their sense of social cohesiveness, and with their face-to-face group structure. The Amish children manifest trusting rather than alienated relationships and therefore possess psychological strengths that should not be undermined by an educational system that is primarily competitive, analytical, and technologically oriented. They will flourish when the educational subject matter is presented in a style that is consistent with the positive aspects of their world view. This does not mean that they are getting a second-class education nor that they are being prevented from entering the mainstream of American culture; rather their psychological strength is being maintained while they learn facts and an approach to education that will make it possible, should the individual so choose, to continue his education beyond that offered by his own culture.

The Amish children scored lowest in vocabulary and language on the standardized tests. This suggests, among other explanations, a strong tie to oral values in contrast to literary values in their tradition. The limitations in vocabulary and language as measured by standardized tests may be seen as a part of the larger value pattern of nonexposure to the world and is thus part of the "good life" as defined by the Amish culture. It is an aspect of separation from the world. Aside from any ambiguity in the standardized tests that might account for Amish score performance, we must remember that the Amish demand economy of words, slowness in mastering content, and prohibitions against showmanship in the use of vocabulary. Moderation is a life-principle learned throughout the school years; consideration for others outweighs individual achievement.

Our findings suggest a similarity to children studied in other subcultures whose cognitive style is primarily relational rather than analytical (Cohen 1969:842). If these children are to develop marketable skills, they will require, according to Friedenberg (1970:43), instruction by techniques that emphasize drill and rote learning. Drill and rote learning, especially when carried on in a group, are more of a social activity than is analysis or abstract thinking, which is primarily an individual exercise. Children whose world view is based on an oral tradition and a personal appropriation of group memory and group wisdom rather than on scientific analysis and abstract reasoning should not be deprived of learning methods that utilize memorization. It is not that these children are without curiosity, it is rather that their curiosity is prescientific and is often social and practical rather than technological. Certainly within our culture we have need for those who appropriate old skills as well as for those who invent new ones.

The Amish are basically nonexploitative of either individuals or of natural resources. People are not conceived of in terms of work units or manpower, nor is the physical environment believed to be inexhaustible. Social responsibility extends beyond concern for their people to stewardship of the land. They consciously reject the goals of a society that is "hung up on competitive achievement" (Friedenberg 1970:43) and that stresses efficiency above all else. Manipulation and power over others is denounced; nurturing and the bearing of one another's burdens is encouraged.

PRACTICAL AND VISCERAL LEARNING

The wisdom of the ages is better imparted to children by example than by precept. Therefore the Amish feel very strongly that the teachers in their schools should be participating members of the Amish culture. Since the Amish limit formal education of their members, although they encourage informal education, the Amish teachers do not meet state certification standards. The Amish with few exceptions reject certified teachers—teachers who have completed prescribed college course requirements—because teachers who meet state standards generally prefer the scientific method of analysis to the prescientific oral tradition. They are not qualified by Amish standards and are incapable of teaching Amish children by the example of their lives. Because of the limited formal training of Amish teachers, there has been widespread concern about the quality of the teaching the children are receiving in the Amish schools. Our findings show that even though the teachers are not state-certified, they are in fact qualified, and that the children are given a satisfactory education in the basic academic skills. (In their own schools, the Amish tested higher than the children in rural public schools in spelling, arithmetic, and word usage.) In addition, their education admirably prepares them for life as Amishmen in the twentieth century. The children aspire to the occupational roles available to them; they succeed in these roles and enjoy their chosen vocations. Their education enables them to be both Amishmen and Americans—to attain a comfortable identity as they perpetuate their distinctive way of life.

All elementary school children need role models. Learning is enhanced when the children and the teacher can identify with each other. A primary reason the Amish schools are successful is that the Amish teacher and children understand one another and identify with each other. There is an important distinction between understanding and identification: understanding is cerebral and identification is visceral. Many educators may have the capacity to understand the needs of a community and the willingness to meet these needs, but fail to identify with either the community or the children. Where the social class (or culture) or the community and the teacher are similar, both understanding and identification are likely to exist. When teachers work in communities or in a culture whose dominant values they either hold or respect, and whose child-training practices they approve and tend to follow themselves, they are better able to teach effectively, to serve as examples to the children, and to help the children to grow culturally. Where middle-class teachers confront lower-class children and parents or where there are sharp differences in culture, ethnicity, or race, understanding may be possible but identification is halfhearted or largely unsuccessful. The oft-repeated notion of having the best teachers in the poorer schools may be pointless except where both the cerebral and visceral ability of the teachers is taken into account. To teach well, the teacher must be able to accept her pupils' need for cultural persistence as well as for cultural change.

The concept of "qualified teacher" in addition to that of "certified teacher" should be considered for schools serving other cultural groups. African-American, Indian and Chicano teachers might also be incorporated into the local school system to help make the education relevant to the child being educated, to establish an atmosphere of respect between the teacher and the pupil, and to develop the vital parent-teacher relationship that has repeatedly been demonstrated to be essential for the effective education of the child. Individuals from the community might teach such culturally specialized skills as silverworking, indigenous music, legends, and minority cultural history. In other words, people with little formal education should be in certain cases welcomed into the classroom and acknowledged not only as satisfactory teachers, but as superior teachers. Teacher certification as generally practiced is too narrow, for it excludes those individuals who may be best qualified to identify with and teach children of culturally divergent groups. Teacher certification often excludes those individuals who can give the children enough of their own culture to make them sufficiently secure to be open to education for change.

APPRENTICESHIP TRAINING

Apprenticeship is a means of imparting specialized knowledge to a new generation of practitioners (Coy 1989:xi). It is the rite of passage that transforms novices into experts. Attitudes and skills that cannot be easily communicated by conventional means can be learned through apprenticeship. Learning by apprenticeship allows implicit knowledge to be acquired through observation and experience. Learning by doing not only relates to skills but also to the means of structuring economic and social relationships between the novice and the master of a vocation.

The Amish use a system of vocational training for their adolescents that takes them outside the school, into the world of adults, and into the life of the community in order that the young people may learn vocational roles as well as vocational skills. These are not "made" jobs, for the community needs their labor and is acutely conscious of its responsibility for training the young people. In some communities the students spend half a day a week in school under the direction of a teacher and four and a half days working in a modified apprentice system, generally under the direction of their parents. They are learning technological skills in a social context as participants in the economy of the community. While working on a family farm, Amish children of high-school age learn not only how to perform a task, such as how to cut silage, but also when to cut it and how to integrate the cutting of the silage into all the other work that is required of the vocation "farmer." They also learn wider community work roles by helping in threshing rings and at cornhuskings, getting ready for church, and helping care for neighbors' children. The young people have practice interacting with the various people with whom they will work throughout their adult lives. Of great importance to the success of the Amish vocational training is that the vocational expectations of the young people coincide with the vocational opportunities available to them.

Adolescents learn faster by actual participation than by talking about participation. Working at real jobs outside the school walls helps students to envision their adult roles and their place in society. Were a program similar to the Amish vocational school program to be implemented by a public school, the selection of individuals to direct and train the students might pose a problem, for in our mobile and diversified society the children's parents would rarely be the ideal individuals to direct the training. It would also be more difficult to find meaningful work that was integrated into the community economy. A directed apprentice program could enable students to master the etiquette of the job by learning how to behave in relation to superiors and towards co-workers. With such a vocational program the

Young farmers attending a horse auction acquire knowledge by observation and experience. (Lancaster New Era photo, by Martin Heisey.)

young person could develop a realistic concept of the job role for which he was training; he would learn both the technological and the social aspects of his work.

There is an underlying assumption in the United States that academic achievement is the most important object of all schooling and that if the school reform does not affect academic achievement, it is worthless. Despite these assumptions "there is little evidence that academic competence is critically important to adults in most walks of life" (Jencks 1969). Most employers will not hire dropouts for reasons other than academic incompetence. It is for moral, social, and emotional reasons. Too often the dropouts do not get to work on time; they cannot be counted on to do a careful job, cannot be trusted with other people's property or goods, cannot get along well with others in the office or plant, and cannot learn new skills needed for the job. The teaching of more history, verbal skills, or science will not suffice. What is needed is training in responsibility, self-discipline, and self-respect. These nonacademic traits can be taught in an apprentice system as well as in a classroom.

In Pennsylvania, the Amish system of vocational education combines on-the-job training with academic work under a teacher's guidance and with peer group interaction at classes that meet half a day a week. The various social and cultural needs of the adolescent are met by this program. The young adult has an opportunity to relate to his family, his boss, his teacher, and his peers while contributing to the economic life of his community.

SMALL SCALE

One of the methods by which the Amish teach and maintain social cohesion is by keeping the units of the church and the school small, so that both function on a face-to-face basis without dependence on administration. The Amish simplify their life by keeping their institutions on a human rather than a bureaucratic scale. Their personal relationships involve repeated encounters and generally persist over a long period of time. There is a homogeneity of belief that makes consensus possible. When homogeneity is lost, the church or the school divides into smaller units. Within the Amish school the children are in a single group in which everyone knows everyone else, in which every family knows every other family, and in which the teacher not only knows all the children but also all the children's families. Often the children have the same teacher for several years and her life is intermixed with theirs in the life of the church and the community. Such a school is not merely a place of instruction, but is part of the children's whole life and culture. It is an ideal environment in which to transmit cultural attitudes. The teacher is in a good position to encourage moral thoughtfulness and to lead frank discussions of social behavior when problems of meanness, fighting, or lying occur.

Young children seem to be able to learn most easily in an environment where they feel secure and where they are accepted as individuals. In describing the First Street School, Dennison (1969:12,29), pointed out that the small face-to-face nature of the school diminished anxiety. He makes a plea for the establishment of "mini-schools" that are characterized by intimacy and small scale. Although the teaching methods used in the First Street School were totally different from those used in Amish schools, both types of school are characterized by intimate contacts among children and teachers and a real respect for individuality. Children learn social cohesion by experience within a socially cohesive group.

It should be pointed out that education for social cohesion and education for technological competence need not be opposed to one another, although in school practice it sometimes appears that they are. The styles in public education change with the needs—or imagined needs—of the surrounding culture. Thus the emphasis moved from social adjustment as urbanization spread to technological competence as a response to Sputnik. Now there appears to be a need to reassess some of our educational practices in the light of man's relation to man, his relation to his physical environment, the relation of one cultural group to another, and children's understanding of themselves. Although the Amish schools have largely rejected training in abstract reasoning, perhaps we can learn something from them in the fields of interpersonal relationship—nonexploitation of the environment, dedication to a principled world view, and the creation of an environment protected from shoddiness, violence, and treachery in which to nurture children and imbue them with a sense of responsibility for others.

It is obvious that the Amish will not tolerate the removal of their children to a distance from their homes, where they are placed in large groups with narrow age limits, taught skills that are useless to their way of life, and exposed to values and attitudes antithetical to their own. These conditions develop when schools become large and bureaucratic. Then the Amish withdraw or migrate, for they say "it is better to suffer than to compromise." They establish their own schools, and when that is not possible, they move to other states or even to other countries. The Amish are determined to raise their children to thrive on cooperation and humility, rather than competition and pride of achievement.

In the United States the Old Order Amish are granted a tenuous permission, revokable virtually at the whim of the state superintendents, to maintain their own schools. It is national public opinion, not school officials or state legislatures, that enables the Amish to keep their own schools in operation.

A COMFORTABLE IDENTITY

The Amish emphasize education for persistence. Although the Amish show remarkable resourcefulness in adjusting to the changing culture around them, it is a resourcefulness that enables them to maintain their traditional world view and their traditional way of life rather than to bring these into line with the changing technical and social environment. In the absence of definite proof, the old way is considered to be better than the new way.

The Amish school is benevolently authoritarian; the teacher is the shepherd, the children are the flock. The teacher's authority is natural, for it derives from the parents and the community. Authority is not arbitrary and is not based on intimidation. The Amish children are taught that there are right answers for all questions, even if they or the teacher may not know them. There is right and wrong, and it is more important to do what is morally right than it is to win acclaim, popularity, or riches, or to survive physically. In order to decide what is morally right, one looks to the Bible, the *Ordnung,* and the elders—to the wisdom of the ages rather than to pronouncements of modern science.

Within the clearly defined and relatively narrow boundaries of the culture and the school there is considerable freedom and a comfortable identity. There is a certain richness and diversity of experience in the small Amish school with its face-to-face organization and its long-term intimate relationships. Respect accrues to each individual if he does not exceed the boundaries. Thus, if a child is not good at softball or is slow at mastering spelling, he is not rejected or looked down on. Variation in ability is realistically accepted. Patterns of decision-making and authority are clear. Many decisions are made by the teacher as representative of the community, but when the children are invited to participate in decision making, their views are respected. The basic conditions for education are possible with very limited educational equipment when the elements of trust, respect, and acceptance of honest needs and wishes are shared by the teacher and the pupils.

The Amish have been able to stop, at least temporarily, the onslaught of the large school and its associated values. They have scant legal protection and little guarantee other than public sentiment for the maintenance of their schools, in which their children are learning the skills and attitudes required of their culture. Were it not for the Amish appeal to religious freedom and nostalgic American values, their communities would long since have been forced out of their pastoral "poverty" into the economic mainstream, where they would either have contributed more to the gross national product or would have added to the welfare rolls already swelled with unhappy individuals drifting between the culture they no longer have and the middle-class culture they do not fully embrace. Instead the Amish have been able, through community discipline, community support of their members, and by the

Decorative arts, including quilts, are made by the family and groups of friends and relatives, often as wedding gifts but also for a growing commercial market. (Photo by Dick Brown.)

careful protection and nurturing of their children, to maintain cultural continuity and cultural integrity, to remain a discreet minority, steadfast to their own vision of the good life.

A MODEL FOR THE POST-INDUSTRIAL AGE

Fifty years ago, the Amish were viewed by many as an obdurate sect living by oppressive customs and exploiting the labor of their children. Thirty-five years ago Amish parents were sent to jail for not allowing their children to go to school beyond eighth grade. They were viewed with disdain as a group who renounced both modern conveniences and the American dream of progress and affluence. In contrast, today the Amish are esteemed by many as meticulous farmers, practicing the virtues of thrift and hard work, and as islands of sanity in a culture obsessed with rampant technology and an extravagant standard of living. Growing disillusion with the materialistic and growth-oriented philosophies that have dominated the values and goals of Western societies has stimulated a search for new models of social organization that offer a good life without exploiting either people or the environment.

Thomas Foster (1981) has suggested that the Amish have avoided the pitfalls of industrial society and provided a model for the coming post-industrial era. The community of the future should be environmentally and ecologically conscious and concerned, spiritually alert, and opposed to waste and consumerism. And Olshan

(1980:160–186) has described the Amish as innovators in rural community development. An ecologically sound society, according to Schumacher (1970), is a "conserver society" characterized by self government, a degree of community self-sufficiency, escape from fossil fuel dependency, population decentralization, and freedom from consumer-oriented education. Schumacher emphasized the importance of people-centered technologies for the existence of a balanced and humane social order. These decentralized technologies should be designed to serve the needs of small producers over the needs of big industrialists. Appropriate technologies should be labor- rather than energy-intensive, cheap enough to be accessible to the masses, and not violate the need for creativity, or pose a threat to the environment. Work should be a joyful activity benefiting body and soul. Not every new labor-saving invention should be viewed as a blessing. The Amish, some have argued, provide a model of the "frugal community" of the future.

For over two centuries the Amish have striven to maintain their ideology, including a preference for plain "unworldly" living in a rural environment, large families, and a belief in tilling the soil without depleting its fertility. The Amish practice certain restraints to protect the land from exploitation. By exercising stewardship, or care for the land they also make their farms attractive and orderly. Their small, diversified farms are more like large gardens rather than corporate factories. They farm not purely to make money, but to enjoy life with their children, who also learn how to enjoy work while sustaining a viable way of life. The Amish are selective in choosing the areas in which they settle and the machines that will

Pre-school children riding in a buggy that complies with state laws regarding licensing, lighting, and display of slow moving vehicle emblem. This Indiana buggy is also equipped with white reflective tape. (Photo by Mike Hanley.)

influence their lives. They do not accept the "worldly" slogan that the bigger machines are better nor that all labor-saving devices improve life. By restraining big technology and consumer-oriented education, by rejecting political involvement in the outside world and by emphasizing their religiously-based lifestyle, they have minimized some of the characteristics of the larger society such as personal alienation, haste, waste, distraction, violence, and disintegration of the family.

The difference between Amish farmlands and large midwestern factory-like farms has been considered by Wendell Berry (1981:250) to be "as great as that between a desert and an oasis." In midwestern farming country good houses are going to ruin, pasture fences have been removed, machines too large for doorways are left in the weather, windbreaks and woodlots have disappeared, and small schoolhouses and churches are left deserted or are used for storing grain. In areas where the Amish are settled there is diversified farming on small holdings. Livestock is integrated with field cropping and cottage industry. Each member of the family has a productive role in the total enterprise. Amish farming practices have been ignored, Berry believes, because biological, cultural and community benefits are too complex for standard bookkeeping procedures.

The Amish are not relics of a bygone era. They have maintained their identity by exhibiting great adaptability in a rapidly changing world; an adaptability vividly demonstrated by their ability to create and maintain their own system of education, an adaptability that has enabled them to live within the larger culture while rejecting specific aspects of that culture. Though not a model for all of society, the Amish demonstrate a different, yet successful way to be modern.

Bibliography and References Cited

AMMON, RICHARD, 1989, *Growing Up Amish*. New York: Atheneum.

ARMSTRONG, PENNY, and SHERYL FELDMAN, 1986, *A Midwife's Story*. New York: Arbor House.

Articles of Agreement Regarding the Indiana Amish Parochial Schools and the Department of Public Instruction. 1984, Gordonville, Pa.: (Indiana Amish State Executive Committee).

BERRY, WENDELL, 1981, *The Gift of Good Land*. San Francisco: North Point Press.

Blackboard Bulletin, The. Aylmer, Ontario: Pathway Publishing Corporation. Published monthly "in the interests of Amish parochial schools." Founded 1957.

BRONFENBRENNER, URIE, 1970, *Two Worlds of Childhood: U.S. and U.S.S.R.* New York: Russell Sage.

BRYER, KATHLEEN B., 1979, "The Amish Way of Death: A Study of Family Support Systems," *American Psychologist* 34 (March):255–61.

BUCHANAN, FREDERICK S., 1967, *The Old Paths: A Study of the Amish Response to Public Schooling in Ohio*. Ph.D. dissertation, Department of Education, Ohio State University.

BYLER, URIA R., 1963, *Our Better Country*. Gordonville, Pa.: Old Order Book Society.

————, 1969, *School Bells Ringing: A Manual for Amish Teachers and Parents*. Aylmer, Ontario: Pathway Publishing Corporation.

COHEN, ROSALIE A., 1969, "Conceptual Styles, Culture Conflict, and Nonverbal Tests of Intelligence," *American Anthropologist* 71:828–856.

COMMAGER, HENRY S., 1962, *Foreword to McGuffey's Sixth Eclectic Reader*. 1879 Edition. New York: Signet Classics.

COY, MICHAEL W., ed., 1989, *Apprenticeship: From Theory to Method and Back Again*. Albany: State University of New York Press.

CRONK, SANDRA L., 1977, "Gelassenheit: The Rites of the Redemptive Process in Old Order Amish and Old Order Mennonite Communities." Ph.D. dissertation, University of Chicago. Excerpts under the same title appear in *Mennonite Quarterly Review* 55 (January 1981):5–44.

DENNISON, GEORGE, 1969, *The Lives of Children: The Story of the First Street School*. New York: Random House.

EDUCATIONAL POLICIES COMMISSION, 1961, *The Central Purpose of Education*. Washington, D.C.: National Educational Association.

ERICKSEN, EUGENE P., J. A. ERICKSEN, J. A. HOSTETLER, and G. E. HUNTING-TON, 1979, "Fertility Patterns and Trends among the Old Order Amish." *Population Studies* 33 (July):255–76.

ERICKSEN, EUGENE P., J. A., ERICKSEN, and J. A. HOSTETLER, 1980, "The Cultivation of the Soil as a Moral Directive: Population Growth, Family Ties, and the Maintenance of Community among the Old Order Amish." *Rural Sociology* 45 (Spring):49–68.

ERICKSON, DONALD A., 1968, "The 'Plain People' & American Democracy," *Commentary,* January, pp. 43–47.

———, 1969, *Public Controls for Non-Public Schools.* Chicago: University of Chicago Press.

ESH, CHRISTIAN G., 1982, *The Beginning and Development of Parochial Special Schools in Lancaster County.* Gordonville, Pa.: Christian G. Esh.

ESH, LEVI A., 1977, "The Amish Parochial School Movement." *Mennonite Quarterly Review* 51 (January):69–75. Reprinted from 1973 *Directory.*

FERSTER, HERBERT V., 1983, "The Development of the Amish School System." *Pennsylvania Mennonite Heritage* 6 (April):7–14.

FISHER, SARA E., and RACHEL K. STAHL, 1986, *The Amish School.* Intercourse, Pa.: Good Books.

FISHMAN, ANDREA, 1988, *Amish Literacy: What and How It Means.* Portsmouth, New Hampshire: Heineman Educational Books.

FOSTER, THOMAS W., 1981, "Amish Society: A Relic of the Past Could Become a Model for the Future." *The Futurist* (December):33–38.

FREED, RUTH S., AND STANLEY A. FREED, 1968, "Family Background and Occupational Goals of School Children of the Union Territory of New Delhi, India," *American Museum Novitates,* No. 2348, October 4. New York: American Museum of Natural History, pp. 1–39.

FREY, J. WILLIAM, 1950, *Pennsylvania Dutch Grammar.* Lancaster, Pa.: Pennsylvania German Folklore Center. Reprint 1981.

———, 1981, *A Simple Grammar of Pennsylvania Dutch.* Lancaster, Pa.: John Baers and Son.

FRIEDENBERG, EDGAR Z., 1970, "The Real Functions of Educational Testing," *Change,* January-February, pp. 43–47.

GOODMAN, MARY E., 1957, "Value, Attitudes, and Concepts of Japanese and American Children," *American Anthropologist* 59:979–999.

Guidelines, In Regards to the Old Order Amish or Mennonite Parochial Schools, 1981, Gordonville, Pa. Old Order Amish Steering Committee 70 pp.

Guidelines for Amish Parochial School Officials of Holmes Wayne and Surrounding Counties. (1990), Millersburg, Ohio: Delegative Committee.

HARRIS, DALE B., 1963, *Children's Drawings as Measures of Intellectual Maturity.* New York: Harcourt, Brace and World, Inc.

———, 1964, "A Cross-Cultural Analysis of Children's Drawings," unpublished manuscript, University Park, Pa.: Pennsylvania State University.

HENRY, JULES, 1963, *Culture against Man.* New York: Random House.

———, 1963, "Spontaneity, Initiative, and Creativity in Suburban Classrooms," in *Education and Culture,* George D. Spindler, ed. New York: Holt, Rinehart and Winston, Inc., pp. 215–233.

HERSHBERGER, NOAH L., 1985, *A Struggle to be Separate*. Orrville, Ohio: Noah L. Hershberger.

HOLT, JOHN, 1964, *How Children Fail*. New York: Pitman.

HOSTETLER, J. A., 1969, *Educational Achievement and Life Styles in a Traditional Society, the Old Order Amish*. Washington, D.C.: U.S. Department of Health, Education and Welfare. Final Report, Project No. 6-1921.

————, 1980, *Amish Society*. Baltimore, Md.: The Johns Hopkins Press. Third ed.

————, 1989, *Amish Roots*. The Johns Hopkins Press.

HOSTETLER, J. A., and G. E. HUNTINGTON, 1980, *The Hutterites in North America*. New York: Holt, Rinehart and Winston, Inc. (Spindler Series.)

HUNTINGTON, GERTRUDE ENDERS, 1956, *Dove at the Window: A Study of an Old Order Amish Community in Ohio*. Ph.D. dissertation, Yale University.

————, 1988, "The Amish Family," In *Ethnic Families in America: Patterns and Variations*, Charles H. Mindel, Robert W. Habenstein and Roosevelt Wright, Jr., eds. Third ed. New York: Elsevier Scientific Publishing.

JENCKS, CHRISTOPHER, 1969, "A Reappraisal of the Most Controversial Educational Document of Our Times," *New York Times Magazine*, August 10, pp. 12ff.

KEIM, ALBERT N., ed., 1975, *Compulsory Education and the Amish: The Right Not to Be Modern*. Boston: Beacon Press.

KLINE, DAVID, 1990, *Great Possessions: An Amish Farmer's Journal*. San Francisco: North Point Press.

KRAYBILL, DONALD B., 1989, *The Riddle of Amish Culture*. Baltimore: The Johns Hopkins Press.

LAPP, CHRIST S., 1991, *Pennsylvania School History: 1690–1990*. Gordonville, Pa.: Published by the author.

LEE, DOROTHY, 1959, *Freedom and Culture*. Englewood Cliffs, N.J.: Prentice-Hall.

————, 1963, "Discrepancies in the Teaching of American Culture," in *Education and Culture*, George D. Spindler, ed. New York: Holt, Rinehart and Winston, Inc.

LITTELL, FRANKLIN H., 1964, *The Origins of Sectarian Protestantism*. New York: Macmillan.

LOOMIS, CHARLES P., and J. ALLAN BEEGLE, 1950, *Rural Social Systems*. Englewood Cliffs, N.J.: Prentice-Hall.

LUTHY, DAVID, 1986, *The Amish in America: Settlements That Failed, 1840–1960*. Aylmer, Ontario: Pathway Publishers.

MILLER, WAYNE, 1969, *A Study of Amish Academic Achievement*. Ph.D. dissertation, Department of Education, University of Michigan.

Minimum Standards for the Amish Parochial or Private Elementary Schools of the State of Ohio as a Form of Regulations. (c. 1957), n.p.

MYERS, ISABEL B., 1962, *The Myers–Briggs Type Indicator*. Princeton, N.J.: Educational Testing Service.

MYERS, ISABEL BRIGGS and PETER BRIGGS MYERS, 1980, *Gifts Differing*. Palo Alto, Ca.: Consulting Psychologists Press, Inc.

NISLEY, JONAS, 1965, *Children's Read, Write, Color, Book*. Baltic, Ohio: Author.

Ohio Legislative Service Commission, 1960, *Sectarian Amish Education*. Columbus, Ohio: Research Report No. 44.

OLSHAN, MARC, 1980, *The Old Order Amish as a Model for Development*. Ph.D. Dissertation, Department of Rural Sociology, Cornell University.

Pathway Publishers, 1970, *Tips for Teachers, A Handbook for Amish Teachers*. Aylmer, Ontario, and Lagrange, Indiana.

Pathway Readers. Aylmer, Ontario: Pathway Publishing Corporation. Titles: *First Steps* (First Grade), *Days Go By* (First Grade), *More Days Go By* (First Grade), *Busy Times* (Second Grade), *More Busy Times* (Second Grade), *Climbing Higher* (Second Grade), *New Friends* (Third Grade), *More New Friends* (Third Grade), *Building Our Lives* (Fourth Grade), *Living Together* (Fifth Grade), *Step by Step* (Sixth Grade), *Seeking True Values* (Seventh Grade), and *Our Heritage* (Eighth Grade).

Pennsylvania Department of Public Instruction, 1955, "Policy for Operation of Home and Farm Projects in Church Organized Schools." Harrisburg, Pa.: October 5.

Regulations and Guidelines for Amish Parochial Schools of Indiana. (1978), Middleberry, Ind.

RODGERS, HARRELL R., 1969, *Community Conflict, Public Opinion and the Law: The Amish Dispute in Iowa*. Columbus, Ohio: Merrill.

SCHOOLAID, 1986, *Schoolteacher's Signposts*. (Schoolaid, 1981, N. Churchtown Road, East Earl, Pa. 17519.) Titles: *Learning Through Sounds, Book 1 and 2, Climbing to Good English*, and *Teacher's Aid Books*.

SCHUMACHER, E. F., 1973, *Small is Beautiful: Economics as if People Mattered*. New York: Harper & Row.

SMUCKER, MERVIN R., 1988, "How Amish Children View Themselves and Their Families: The Effectiveness of Amish Socialization." *Brethren Life and Thought* 33 (Summer):218–36.

SPINDLER, GEORGE D., 1963, *Education and Culture—Anthropological Approaches*. New York: Holt, Rinehart and Winston, Inc.

Standards of the Old Order Amish and Old Order Mennonite Parochial and Vocational Schools of Pennsylvania, 1981, Gordonville, Pa.: Gordonville Print Shop.

STOLL, JOSEPH, 1963, *The Challenge of the Child*. Aylmer, Ontario: Pathway Publishing Corporation (Second edition, 1967).

———, 1965, *Who Shall Educate Our Children?* Aylmer, Ontario: Pathway Publishing Corporation.

———, 1976, *Child Training*. Aylmer, Ontario: Pathway Publishing Corporation.

United States Supreme Court, 1972, *Wisconsin v. Yoder*, No. 70–110.

WELLS, RICHARD D., 1967, *Articles of Agreement Regarding the Indiana Amish Parochial Schools and Department of Public Instruction*. Indianapolis, Ind.: Department of Public Instruction, Richard D. Wells, Superintendent.

WESTERHOFF, JOHN H., 1978, *McGuffey and His Readers*. Milford, Michigan: Mott Media, Inc.

WITTMER, JOE, 1970, "Homogeneity of Personality Characteristics: A Comparison between Old Order Amish and Non-Amish," *American Anthropologist* 72:1063–1068.

ZOOK, NOAH, 1963, *Seeking a Better Country*. Gordonville, Pa.: Old Order Book Society.

Index

Achievement scores, 93–95
Administration. *See* Methods of Teaching
Adolescence. *See* Young People
Adulthood, roles and expectations, 20
Affiliation, church defined, 7
Age stages, listed, 19–20
Aging, acceptance of, 33
Agricultural values, 12
Alternatives, of the Amish community, 46
Ammann, Jacob, as founder, 5; on shunning, 12
Amish school: organization, 51; board, 51; founding of, 37; schedule, 59
Anthropological methods, in this study, 16–17, 96
Apprenticeship training, 114
Attendance (school), 56; after grade eight, 67
Authority: how acquired, 23; and responsibility, 23

Babyhood: stage, 21; handling of, 22
Ball, William B., attorney, 43
Baptism: and membership, 10, 16; obligations of, 31; for life, 10
Barn raising, 28
Benedict, Ruth, on Pueblos, 93
Berger, Chief Justice, cited, 44
Bible-reading, 61, 72
Birth, 21
Blackboard Bulletin, 63, 81
Board members, 51–54
Buildings, 57

Certification, and qualified Amish versus state-certified teachers, 49, 113–114
Childrearing, adult committments to, 20
Children, nature of, 14–15
Children, in custody, 38
Church district: defined, 6; size, 6–7
Cohen, Rosalie, cited on relational types, 75, 112
Cohesion, education for, 111–112
Commager, Henry, on McGuffy Readers, 62
Community: basis of, 9; discipline in, 10; training for, 71; shares values, 11; protects the family values, 11
Compulsory school attendance age, 56
Confrontation, examples of, 37, 40
Conscription, 31, 105
Consolidation: arguments for, 46; objections to, 45
Conversion, role of family and church in, 15
Core values, 8
Cost of building, financial aspects associated with, 54

Courtship, 31
Creation: biblical account of, 8; and stewardship, 13; and farming expertise, 13; and community maintenance, 13
Curriculum: basic subjects taught, 61; texts 61–62; authors of, 62

Death, community response to, 35
Diploma, 50
Discipline, common to all Old Order Amish, 8
Disputes, parental, 87
Dress, of pupils, 87
Dropouts from Amish society, 104
Drawings, of children, 99

Education, as defined by the Amish, 14, 68
Educational goals, 13, 14, 26
Enrollment (school), policy of, 56
Eternity, and accountability for nurture, 16
Evaluation of schools: success of, 109; weaknesses recognized, 70
Evangelism, attitudes towards, 12
Excommunication, of offenders, 12

Fairy tales, objections to, 63
Family: size, 4; household, 6
Father, role of, 24
Fears, loss of children for eternity, 16
Finances, and responsibility of, 54–55
Funerals, 35

Games, at school, 65
Garber, LeRoy, arrest of, 43
GED tests, 68
Gingerich, Eli, quoted on length of school year, 59
Goals of education: general goals, 13–14; and successful schools, 109
Golden Rule, emphasized in classroom, 82, 87
Gordonville Print Shop, 62
Government, and areas of cooperation, 57
Grading, practices of, 83
"Grandfather house," and retirement, 33

Handicapped, schools for, 68, 69
Harris, Dale B., on Draw-A-Man Test, 95
Heating and janitorial work, 65
Hershberger, Henry, spokesman, 38
High school, a dangerous environment, 56
High-low culture context, 75
History of the Amish, 4–5
Holidays, 59
Home schooling, 56

125

INSTRUCTIONAL FILM AVAILABLE: VHS Video Cassette:

The Amish: A People of Preservation. 54 min. Revised 1991. Available from Heritage Productions, 1191 Summeytown Pike, Harleysville, Pa. 19438